Gluten Free Cookbook

"Delicious and nourishing recipes for a gluten-free lifestyle"

By *JENNA CARTER*

Gluten Free Cookbook

© Copyright 2023 - All rights reserved.

This book's contents cannot be copied, duplicated, or transmitted without the publisher's or author's express written consent.

The publisher and author disclaim all liability for any losses, claims, or financial damages resulting from the material in this book. Not in a direct or indirect way.

Legal Notice:

Copyright protects this book. This book is solely meant for individual use. No part of this work may be reproduced, distributed, sold, quoted, or paraphrased without the publisher's or author's consent.

Disclaimer Notice:

Please be aware that the information in this publication is solely meant to be used for amusement and education. We've done everything we can to provide accurate, up-to-date, trustworthy, and comprehensive information. There are no expressed or implied guarantees of any kind. The reader understands that the writer is not providing professional, financial, medical, or legal advice. This book's content was compiled from a number of sources. Please do not undertake any of the practices in this book without first consulting a licensed specialist.

By using the information in this document, the reader acknowledges and agrees that the author shall not be held responsible for any direct or indirect loss resulting from the use of such material, including but not limited to errors, omissions, or inaccuracies.

Table of Contents

Introduction	7
Chapter 1: The Science Behind the Gluten-Free Diet	12
Chapter 2: The Basics of Eating Gluten Free	15
Chapter 3: Embracing a Gluten-Free Lifestyle	24
Chapter 4: Baking Substitutes and Tips	32
Chapter 5: Breakfast Recipes	36
1. Vegetables with Hash Browns	37
2. Waffles with Cinnamon	38
3. Golden Blueberry Muffins	39
4. Fluffy Buttermilk Pancakes	40
5. Buttery Butter Biscuits	42
6. Tasty Oatmeal Raisin Bars	44
7. Cinnamon Vanilla Banana Bread	46
8. Moist Pumpkin Spice Bread	48
9. Coffee and Cream Pops	50
Chapter 6: Lunch Recipes	52
10. Gluten-Free Angel Food Cake	53
11. Gluten-Free Strawberry & Pistachio Olive Oil Cake	55
12. Gluten-Free Thumbprint Cookies	57
13. Chewy Lemon Sugar Cookies	59
14. Peanut Butter Blossoms	61
15. Easy Strawberry Tart	63
16. Lemon Tart	65
17. Chocolate Tart	67
18. Butter Tarts	69
19. Mini S'mores Tarts	70

20. Caramel Apple Tart 72
21. Summer Berry Tortilla Tart 74
22. Gluten-Free Strawberry-Almond Tart 76
23. Gluten-Free Vegan Matcha Mousse Tart 78
24. Cherry-Almond Vanilla Cupcakes 80
25. Lavender-Honey Cupcakes 82
26. Mochaccino Cupcakes 84

Chapter 7: Dinner Recipes   86

27. Italian Sauce 87
28. Pot Roast 89
29. Corned Beef and Cabbage 90
30. BBQ Taco Salad 91
31. Beef Curry 92
32. Beef Stroganoff 93
33. Beef Stew 94
34. Chicken Prepared with Forty-Five Garlic Cloves 96
35. Orange Chicken 97
36. General Tso's Chicken 98
37. Spicy Chicken and Quinoa 99
38. Bourbon Chicken 101
39. Spicy Moroccan Fish 102
40. Lemony Salmon 103
41. Louisiana Jambalaya 104

Chapter 8: Snack Recipes   106

42. Bacon-Wrapped Asparagus, Sweet Peppers, And Green Beans.. 107

43. Creamy Potato Salad... 108

44. Bean Dip.. 110

45. Cucumber Cups With Sun-Dried Tomato And Cream Cheese..112

46. Confetti Tuna In Celery Sticks....................................113

47. Vegetable Dip...114

48. Baked Sweet Potato Wedges With Garlic Aioli....... 115

49. Vegetable Fritters...116

50. Pistachio Cranberry Energy Bites.............................117

51. Spicy Avocado Dip.. 118

52. Sweet-And-Sour Zucchini..119

53. Sweet Potato Fries... 120

54. Okra Fries... 121

55. Potato Sticks...122

56. Zucchini Chips... 123

57. Beet Chips.. 124

58. Beet Greens Chips...125

59. Spinach Chips..126

60. Plantain Chips... 127

Chapter 9: Meal Planning and Batch   128
Chapter 10: Troubleshooting and FAQs   133
Conclusion   140

Introduction

In the bustling symphony of daily life, where time is a precious commodity and culinary choices often become a frenzied race against the clock, there exists a shared sentiment—one that resonates across diverse backgrounds, cultures, and lifestyles. It is the ubiquitous struggle with dietary restrictions, specifically the formidable foe that is gluten. As you stand at the intersection of nourishment and flavor, pondering the seemingly insurmountable challenges of a gluten-free lifestyle, allow me to draw you into the captivating narrative of the "Gluten-Free Cookbook."

Picture this: a kitchen imbued with the tantalizing aroma of freshly baked bread, the kind that conjures childhood memories and beckons with a promise of comfort. Now, imagine being told that such pleasures are forever relegated to the realm of nostalgia due to the omnipresence of gluten intolerance. It's a scenario many of us have encountered, a culinary crossroads where the yearning for a delightful, gluten-laden dish collides head-on with the imperative of a gluten-free existence.

The journey we embark upon within these pages is not just a cookbook; it's a compass guiding you through the labyrinth of gluten-free living, acknowledging the frustrations and misconceptions that have cast a shadow over your culinary endeavors. This is not a mere compilation of recipes but a transformative exploration that transcends the boundaries of dietary restrictions, a testament to the belief that gluten-free living is not a limitation but an invitation to reimagine the culinary landscape.

I understand the nuanced struggles that accompany the quest for gluten-free alternatives. It's not just about substituting wheat flour with its gluten-free counterparts; it's about unraveling the intricacies of taste, texture, and satisfaction that define a truly gratifying meal. It's about navigating the emotional terrain of nostalgia and adapting recipes to accommodate a new reality, all while maintaining the essence of what makes a dish truly exceptional.

In the grand tapestry of gluten-free living, I invite you to recognize this cookbook as more than a collection of recipes—it's a lifeline, a culinary confidante that understands your plight and is committed to turning the tables on the perception of gluten-free as synonymous with bland and uninspiring. This book is designed to be your ally in the kitchen, offering a diverse array of recipes that not only adhere to gluten-free principles but also elevate your dining experience to unprecedented heights.

So, why should you invest your time and culinary aspirations in the "Gluten-Free Cookbook"? Because within these pages, you will uncover the secrets to crafting gluten-free dishes that not only meet the dietary requirements but exceed your expectations in taste, texture, and creativity. This is not a mere survival guide for gluten-free living; it's a celebration of the myriad flavors that thrive within the realm of alternative ingredients.

Throughout this culinary odyssey, you will gain insight into the intricacies of gluten-free flours, discovering their unique characteristics and how they contribute to the palatable symphony of each recipe. From the velvety allure of coconut flour to the hearty depth of sorghum flour, you'll traverse a landscape of possibilities that redefine the boundaries of gluten-free baking and cooking.

Moreover, the "Gluten-Free Cookbook" is more than a repository of recipes; it's a gateway to a mindful and health-conscious approach to eating. We delve into the art of mindful cooking, urging you to be conscious not only of the ingredients you use but also of the nourishment you bestow upon your body. This is a holistic guide that extends beyond the kitchen, promoting a harmonious relationship between your well-being and the food you consume.

As the architect of this culinary voyage, I bring to the table not just a wealth of culinary expertise but a genuine passion for transforming the challenges of gluten-free living into opportunities for culinary exploration. My journey is not one of arbitrary expertise but a personal odyssey through the maze of gluten-free adaptation. I understand the frustration of lackluster alternatives and the joy of stumbling upon that perfect combination of ingredients that turns a dish from merely acceptable to undeniably delightful.

This is the right book for you because, within its pages, you will find a roadmap to culinary liberation—a guide that not only empathizes with your challenges but empowers you to embrace gluten-free living with enthusiasm. The recipes are not dictated by a sense of deprivation but fueled by the sheer joy of creating meals that are not just suitable for a gluten-free lifestyle but an absolute delight to the senses.

As you embark on this gastronomic journey, envision not just a cookbook but a companion, a trusted advisor in your culinary exploits. The "Gluten-Free Cookbook" is an ode to the culinary enthusiast within you, an assurance that gluten-free living is not a compromise but an avenue for boundless creativity and indulgence. So, let the adventure begin, and may your kitchen be a canvas for the vibrant palette of gluten-free possibilities that awaits you within these pages.

Gluten Free Cookbook

Chapter 1: The Science Behind the Gluten-Free Diet

Not only has the gluten-free diet gained popularity in recent years among people who have been diagnosed with health disorders that are related to gluten, but it has also gained favor among people who are looking for potential health benefits. This chapter investigates the scientific rationale behind the gluten-free diet, illuminating the advantages of adhering to such a diet as well as the underlying health issues that are linked to gluten.

Benefits of a Gluten-Free Diet

Avoiding the protein gluten, which can be found in grains like wheat, barley, and rye, is a key component of the gluten-free diet. Gluten is a protein that many people really need, but for others it presents a number of challenges. One of the most significant advantages of adhering to a gluten-free diet is the function it plays in the management of celiac disease. Celiac disease is an autoimmune illness in which the consumption of gluten results in damage to the small intestine. This damage can be quite severe. People who have celiac disease can reduce the severity of their symptoms and hasten the process of intestinal repair if they adhere to a diet that does not contain gluten.

Some people choose to live a gluten-free diet not because they have celiac disease but because they are sensitive to gluten in general. Gluten sensitivity is not the same as celiac disease, which involves an autoimmune reaction, but it can induce symptoms that are very similar to celiac disease, such as digestive problems, exhaustion, and headaches. In situations like these, avoiding gluten can help ease discomfort and enhance general health and wellbeing.

In addition, there are people who do not have illnesses that are specifically related to gluten who opt to follow a gluten-free diet for reasons relating to their overall health. They believe that lowering or eliminating gluten intake can lead to better digestion, higher levels of energy, and improved cognitive function. Even though studies on these benefits are still being conducted, there is some anecdotal evidence that supports favorable outcomes for particular people.

Overview of Gluten-Related Health Conditions

Examining the health problems that are linked to gluten consumption in greater detail is necessary in order to comprehend the scientific rationale behind the gluten-free diet. As was noted before, celiac disease is a genetic autoimmune illness that affects around 1 percent of the world's population. Gluten causes people with celiac disease to have an immune system that assaults the small intestine in error, which results in inflammation and damage to the intestinal lining.

On the other hand, gluten sensitivity does not involve an immunological reaction like that which is seen in celiac disease. However, the symptoms can be just as crippling in their own right. In addition to non-digestive symptoms including headaches, joint pain, and exhaustion, digestive difficulties like bloating, diarrhea, and abdominal pain are prevalent. Gluten sensitivity, in contrast to celiac disease, does not cause the same degree of damage to the small intestine as does celiac disease.

In order to diagnose these disorders, a medical evaluation is required, during which blood tests, genetic testing, and even, in rare instances, an intestinal biopsy may be performed. It is essential for people who are suffering symptoms to seek the advice of medical specialists in order to receive an appropriate diagnosis and direction for the management of their diet.

Navigating the Gluten-Free Lifestyle

Avoiding obvious sources of gluten, such as bread and pasta, is only part of what is required to follow a diet that is gluten-free. Gluten can be found in some surprising locations, including condiments, processed foods, and even some cosmetics. Reading product labels carefully becomes an essential ability for people who are embarking on a gluten-free diet.

Because gluten-free alternatives, such as flours produced from rice, almonds, or coconut, are now readily available to consumers, it is now much simpler for people to consume items they are accustomed to eating without jeopardizing their health. However, it is crucial to keep in mind that not all items that do not contain gluten are created equal, and some of them may be deficient in essential nutrients. It is recommended that those who are adhering to a gluten-free diet concentrate their attention on naturally gluten-free whole foods such as fruits, vegetables, proteins that are low in fat, and gluten-free grains such as quinoa and rice.

The science behind the gluten-free diet is rooted in the understanding of celiac disease and gluten sensitivity. While crucial for those with diagnosed conditions, the gluten-free lifestyle has gained traction among individuals seeking various health benefits. As with any dietary change, consulting with healthcare professionals is vital to ensure proper diagnosis, management, and a balanced approach to nutrition in the pursuit of a gluten-free lifestyle.

Chapter 2: The Basics of Eating Gluten Free

A gluten-free diet is one that many people choose to follow for a variety of reasons. Some individuals have high expectations that they will achieve their weight loss, mental clarity, relief from gastrointestinal disorders, or stabilization of mood swings goals. Others look for a treatment that does not include the use of medication for their child's cognitive or behavioral concerns. Gluten-free is often used interchangeably with the word "healthy" among many people. Gluten-free living, on the other hand, can be the difference between life and death for people who have been diagnosed with celiac disease or an allergy to wheat.

The Celiac Disease Foundation estimates that three million people in the United States are living with celiac disease, of which 83 percent have not been properly identified. Consider getting tested to see if you have celiac disease before you start following a gluten-free diet to avoid the symptoms of the disease. If you do have the condition, staying away from gluten in any form for the rest of your life is an absolute need.

Regardless of the factors that led you to decide to eliminate gluten from your diet, you will need to be vigilant and committed in order to avoid ingesting the protein that is difficult to spot. This book will become an invaluable resource for you if you are new to preparing gluten-free meals since it will teach you how to properly stock a gluten-free pantry, carefully read nutrition labels, buy on a budget, and appreciate all of the great foods that are naturally gluten free.

What Is Gluten?

Gluten is a mixture of two proteins called gliadin, which is a prolamin protein, and glutenin, which is a glutelin protein. Both of these proteins are found naturally in some grains.

Gluten causes damage to the lining of the small intestines in people who have celiac disease, which prevents the body from absorbing nutrients in the right manner. This information comes from the Celiac Disease Foundation. The Center for Celiac Research believes that approximately one percent of the population is affected by celiac disease. However, it warns that a significantly greater population may be impacted by non-celiac gluten sensitivity, which could affect at least six percent of the population.

Gluten can induce a wide variety of symptoms in those who are sensitive to it but do not have celiac disease. Some of these symptoms include, but are not limited to, constipation, diarrhea, joint stiffness and discomfort, exhaustion, brain fog, and headaches. There are a number of hypotheses floating about as to why this is the case, with the most widely accepted explanation being that modern gluten is difficult to digest. As a consequence of this, it causes irritation to the digestive system, contributes to increased inflammation throughout the body, and calls for additional energy to be processed. Following a diet that excludes gluten has been shown to improve one's energy levels and provide relief from a variety of these unfavorable symptoms for many people.

Guidelines for Following a Gluten-Free Diet

Stay away from cereals including wheat, barley, rye, and triticale because they contain gluten.

Stay away from items like oats that have a high potential for gluten contamination unless the packaging clearly states that they are gluten free.

Steer clear of foods that contain common wheat elements like bulgur, durum flour, farina, graham flour, kamut, semolina, and spelt. These foods should be avoided.

Toasters, cutting boards, and any other equipment or serving dishes used in the preparation of food should be treated with extreme caution in order to prevent the spread of contamination. Even a tiny piece can be enough to set off an allergic reaction in some people.

When you go grocery shopping for items that do not contain gluten, give yourself plenty of time to peruse product labels and reacquaint yourself with the layout of the store.

Make sure to check with your pharmacist to ensure that the prescription drugs you use do not contain any gluten. (It is highly improbable that the medications themselves contain gluten; however, some pills are held together by substances known as excipients, and these excipients may contain gluten or be made of compounds that include gluten.)

The Celiac Disease Foundation advises, "When in doubt, go without," as their motto states. It is safer not to eat French fries than it is to expose yourself to gluten.

It will take some time for you to figure out what your body needs in order to be healthy and adjust to a lifestyle that does not involve gluten, so be patient with yourself during this process. Consult with a qualified dietician or sign up for a support group offered in your area for those who must avoid gluten in their diet.

The Obvious and Not-So-Obvious Sources of Gluten

The vast majority of individuals are aware that anything made with wheat flour will inherently include gluten. Gluten, on the other hand, can be found in a surprising number of hidden locations, most notably in processed meals that contain lengthy ingredient lists. In addition to removing the obvious sources of the problem, you should check the ingredient lists of all the items you eat to ensure that they do not include any derivatives.

Foods that typically contain gluten:

- Bread
- Cakes
- Cereals
- Cookies
- Crackers
- Matzo
- Muffins
- Pasta
- Pies

Just Because It's Gluten Free Doesn't Mean It's Healthy

The terms "low fat" and "healthy" started to be used interchangeably in the 1980s. "Low-fat" began to show up on a lot of different goods, such as soups, salad dressings, biscuits, and chocolates. The flavor had to come from someplace, even though the dishes had less fat and, in certain cases, less calories. And where had it originally come from? Corn is the source of corn syrup, corn syrup solids, modified food starch, and high-fructose corn syrup. You now have corn goods, in case you wanted any more. Not exactly what you would describe as healthful.

The gluten-free food business has experienced a boom in recent years due to the perception among many consumers—many of whom do not really have a medical necessity to follow a gluten-free diet—that gluten-free products are healthier than those that contain gluten. As a result, the market for gluten-free foods is expanding.

Again, something has to be done to make up for the flavor and texture that are lost when gluten is removed from normally gluten-containing foods. The ingredients listed on a box of gluten-free cake mix include sugar, rice flour, cocoa powder, potato starch, modified tapioca starch, black cocoa, xanthan gum, emulsifier (rice starch, polyglycerol esters of fatty acids, mono- and diglycerides of fatty acids), and leavening (sodium acid pyrophosphate, sodium bicarbonate, cornstarch, mono-calcium phosphate). There is a lot to consider!

As you can see, sugar and processed carbs are used in place of flour in these gluten-free baked goods. Thus, it is imperative to evaluate gluten-free goods according to the caliber of the ingredients they include, much like one should evaluate low-fat foods that gained popularity in the 1980s. Stated differently, a prepared food does not automatically qualify as "healthy" just because it does not include gluten.

What should you check for on the box when you're shopping for gluten-free meals?

First, ascertain the sugar content. While sugar could have a place in a generally healthy diet, it most definitely shouldn't be the main element in gluten-free snacks or desserts.

Second, since not all gluten-free flours are created equal, you should look into substitutes for the flour you are currently using. Select flours with the highest protein content, lowest carbohydrate content, and lowest glycemic index, such as almond flour, garbanzo-fava flour (a mixture of ground fava beans and chickpeas), and coconut flour.

Lastly, you may want to consider staying away from the gluten-free food area completely. Even if the product package says it is gluten-free, processed foods shouldn't make up the bulk of your diet. Instead, choose for whole foods that are inherently gluten-free, like fruits, vegetables, nuts, meat, poultry, and seafood.

Gluten-free alternatives

Going gluten-free does not mean that you have to give up all forms of bread and pasta. Here are some available choices:

Bread: Gluten-free bread often includes egg whites, brown rice flour, oil, potato starch, tapioca starch, sugar or honey, and leavening agents as some of its ingredients. You can create French toast with it instead of conventional wheat bread, use it to keep the moisture in meatballs, bread, fish, or meat, or incorporate it into any other dish in which bread is often used. Gluten-free loaves are typically more expensive than breads that contain wheat, typically costing roughly twice as much for a loaf.

Gluten-free pasta is typically produced using corn, brown rice, quinoa, or some combination of these three ingredients. The majority have approximately 200 calories and 4 grams of protein per each serving size of 2 ounces. Pastas made from corn and quinoa each have approximately 4 grams of fiber, but pasta made from brown rice has only 1 gram of fiber. The consistency of brown rice pasta is often described as being chewier and more mushy. Prices can be significantly lower than those for wheat-based pasta, depending on the manufacturer, but they can also range much higher.

Flour: Gluten-free flours have varied degrees of nutrition, and it's possible that you'll need to use more than one type of gluten-free flour in order to recreate the flavor and texture of your favorite baked goods. Almond flour, arrowroot powder, brown rice flour, coconut flour, garbanzo-fava flour, potato starch, sorghum flour, and tapioca starch are examples of common flour alternatives. The gluten-free flour alternatives that are available, almond flour has the highest nutrient density since it contains protein, vitamin E, and monounsaturated fats in relatively high proportions. Unfortunately, in addition to being the most calorically dense and expensive option, it also has the highest price tag.

If you need gluten-free alternatives that are lower in sugar, starches, or refined carbs, you might want to consider using spaghetti squash or shirataki noodles (found in Asian grocery stores) as pasta substitutes. You should also look for breads that are made with ancient grains like amaranth and millet or seeds like chia seeds and flaxseeds. Both of these types of ingredients are gluten-free.

Chapter 3: Embracing a Gluten-Free Lifestyle

When it comes to making choices about our nutrition, we are constantly inundated with information, fads, and trends, all of which have the potential to leave us feeling overwhelmed. In recent years, the gluten-free diet has emerged as a popular dietary choice option that has garnered a lot of attention. Some people view it as a personal preference, while others consider it to be a prerequisite for their health. I will go into the subject of gluten, its affects on health, and the reasons why some individuals opt to avoid it in this chapter.

Understanding Gluten: The Culprit

First thing's first: let's get rid of the misconception that gluten is intrinsically unhealthy for you. Gluten is a type of protein that can be found in wheat, rye, and barley, as well as the offspring of these three grains. It plays a crucial role in giving bread and pasta their characteristic chewy and elastic textures. Gluten is not inherently dangerous, however the consumption of gluten may have negative consequences on the health of those who ingest it.

Celiac Disease: The Silent Intruder

Let's say for the sake of argument that your immune system has misidentified your own body as an enemy and is now waging a full-scale war on the lining of your intestinal tract. The unfortunate reality is that this holds true for the majority of people who have celiac disease. People who have celiac disease are more likely to get autoimmune symptoms if they consume gluten. Consuming gluten in the small intestine of a person who suffers from celiac disease might set off a chain reaction of inflammation. This inflammation has the potential to bring on a wide variety of serious health problems over time.

The tale of my good buddy Sarah is still fresh in my mind. She had been dealing with unexplained stomach problems for years, during which time she felt fatigued and suffered from recurrent diarrhea. After a plethora of visits to the doctor and testing, the only outcome was a diagnosis of celiac disease that was ultimately reached by a conscientious practitioner. The start of Sarah's journey to a gluten-free diet was a turning point in her life. Within a short period of time, she saw significant improvements in both her energy levels and her gastrointestinal issues. It's remarkable to see the transformation.

Gluten Sensitivity: A Grey Area

Negative reactions to gluten are not necessarily caused by celiac disease in all cases. Certain people suffer from a gluten sensitivity that is not caused by celiac disease (NCGS). People who suffer with NCGS have symptoms that are comparable to those of celiac disease, but they do not have the immune response or the intestinal damage that are typical of celiac disease.

Imagine you ate a great slice of pizza, and then a short while after you felt bloated, gassy, and quite uncomfortable. This is the reality for a great number of individuals who have NCGS. It is a real phenomenon, despite the fact that it is not as well understood as celiac disease. People who have NCGS and follow a diet that is free of gluten frequently experience a dramatic reduction in the severity of their symptoms.

Wheat Allergies: An Immediate Reaction

Wheat allergies are in a league of their own when it comes to the gamut of symptoms that can be caused by gluten. In contrast to celiac disease and NCGS, wheat allergies cause an immediate immune response. This can manifest itself in a variety of ways, including rashes, difficulty breathing, and in the most severe cases, anaphylaxis. Those who have problems digesting gluten or who are allergic to wheat must steer clear of these foods at all costs in order to prevent possibly lethal reactions.

The Gluten-Free Solution

After going over the many medical issues that call for a gluten-free diet, you may be asking why it is absolutely necessary to adhere to this dietary restriction. The answer can be found in the fact that people who suffer from these disorders are more susceptible to the adverse effects that gluten can have.

People who have celiac disease are more likely to experience significant intestinal damage and a wide range of symptoms when they consume even minute amounts of gluten. These symptoms include abdominal pain, diarrhea, exhaustion, and skin rashes. In the long term, celiac disease that is not treated can result in malnutrition, osteoporosis, and an increased risk of developing certain cancers. For some individuals, adhering to a gluten-free diet is quite literally a matter of life and death.

Even though NCGS is not as life-threatening as celiac disease, the symptoms it causes can nevertheless have a significant impact on a person's quality of life. After converting to a gluten-free diet, you may see improvements in gastrointestinal issues, headaches, and overall tiredness.

Last but not least, avoiding gluten is absolutely necessary for those who suffer from a wheat allergy. It could quite literally be the difference between life and death.

Should You Jump on the Gluten-Free Bandwagon, or Is It Just a Fad?

The gluten-free diet has seen significant growth in popularity over the past few years; nevertheless, many people still view it more as a fashion statement than a genuine necessity for their health. Critics contend that a large number of people are jumping on the gluten-free bandwagon for no valid cause, which is contributing to misconceptions about the health benefits of this diet.

It is absolutely necessary, in order to find a solution to this issue, to differentiate between people who avoid gluten in their diet due to health concerns and those who do so as a lifestyle choice. Being gluten-free isn't necessarily beneficial for your health if you don't have celiac disease, NCGS, or an allergy to wheat. These conditions are rare. In point of fact, a good number of gluten-free food options are lacking in vital elements like fiber and protein.

However, it is important to emphasize that a diet free of gluten does not always have to be devoid of nutrients or health benefits. Fruits and vegetables, in addition to nutritious grains that are naturally free of gluten and include quinoa and rice, could be emphasized. Those who are interested in eating healthier in general or reducing their consumption of carbohydrates that have been processed will benefit from this as well.

Possible Advantages to Your Health Associated with Making the Switch to a Gluten-Free Diet

Even while a gluten-free diet is not a cure-all, there is reason to believe that adhering to such a diet may give additional health benefits that go beyond the prevention of gluten-related diseases.

People who do not have celiac disease or NCGS but still have digestive difficulties may feel better after eliminating gluten from their diets. This is because gluten causes inflammation in the digestive tract. It's possible that this will result in less pain, gas, and bloating.

Going gluten-free has been shown to assist some individuals in achieving their weight loss goals. This is typically the case because they cut out a significant quantity of items that include gluten that have been processed and that are high in calories, such as baked goods and fried dishes.

Those who have type 1 diabetes may find that becoming gluten-free helps them maintain more stable blood sugar levels by eliminating gluten from their diet. According to the findings of various pieces of study, gluten consumption has been associated to insulin resistance in certain persons.

Decreased Inflammation Inflammation is the root cause of a wide variety of degenerative conditions, including heart disease and arthritis. It has been demonstrated that removing gluten from one's diet can decrease inflammation and enhance energy levels in some people.

Gluten-free diets frequently result in a heightened awareness of the labels on food products and the components they contain. As people become more conscious of what they put into their bodies, it's possible that they'll start to make healthier choices when it comes to eating.

Navigating the Gluten-Free Lifestyle

If you are considering eliminating gluten from your diet, whether for reasons related to your health or due to a choice of your own, there are several actions that you can take that will make the adjustment less difficult.

Put Yourself in Position: Gain an understanding of the types of foods that contain and do not contain gluten. Master the art of reading food labels and become familiar with the many names used for gluten-containing components.

Seek Treatment If you have celiac disease or NCGS, it is important that you seek help from a dietician or a support group that specializes in gluten-related illnesses. They are able to provide helpful guidance and access to useful resources.

Meal Preparation In order for a change in diet to be successful, it requires meticulous planning. To ensure that your meals remain exciting and delectable while adhering to a gluten-free diet, create a meal plan, a shopping list, and try out various gluten-free dishes.

Explore the possibilities of Whole Foods: Instead of placing a heavy reliance on processed gluten-free items, you should strive to incorporate naturally gluten-free whole foods into your diet. Some examples of these foods include fruits, vegetables, lean meats, and grains that are gluten-free.

Be patient, since adjusting to a lifestyle free of gluten might be challenging at first, but the process does become less challenging over time. Be gentle to yourself, and put your attention on the positive things you're doing for the sake of your health.

Common Myths and Misconceptions

Getting rid of gluten from one's diet is accompanied by a number of myths and misunderstandings, just like any other dietary trend. Let us have a look at some of them, including:

Gluten Should Be Avoided by Everyone a Myth: This is not the case at all. If you do not have celiac disease, NCGS, or an allergy to wheat, there is no clinical reason for you to abstain from gluten consumption. It is essential to establish well-informed selections that are based on the particular needs of your health situation.

Even if a product does not contain gluten, having a label stating that it is gluten-free does not guarantee that the product is healthy. Sadly, many of the gluten-free products available have undergone an excessive amount of processing and may even contain additional carbohydrates or fats. Whenever it is possible, opt for meals that are whole and less processed.

Gluten-Free Diets Are a Miracle for Weight Loss: A gluten-free diet may be helpful for some people in their weight loss efforts, but it is not a foolproof solution to the problem. Counting calories and moving more are still the cornerstones of effective weight management.

Being gluten-free does not equate to feeling deprived: There is a widespread misunderstanding that avoiding gluten in one's diet is restrictive and uninteresting. In point of fact, a wide variety of delectable and wholesome gluten-free meals and dishes are available for consumers to select from. Being imaginative and trying new things is the best way to experience a wide range of cuisines.

In conclusion, the decision to give up gluten is a highly personal one that can be impacted by a wide range of factors, such as particular dietary choices and existing health conditions. Although there is no remedy that is guaranteed to work for everyone, it is obvious that certain individuals must eliminate gluten from their diets in order to improve their health. Those who suffer from celiac disease, NCGS, or wheat allergies should adopt a gluten-free diet and lifestyle as their best option for improving their overall health and well-being.

It is imperative that those who do not have any of these illnesses approach a gluten-free diet with the necessary level of understanding and awareness. It is possible that it has some positive effects on health, but utilizing it won't help you lose weight or improve your health in any way. The foundations of general wellness remain to be a diet that is nutritionally balanced and has an emphasis on eating whole foods.

In the end, regardless of whether you choose to steer clear of gluten or not, it is essential to put your own wellbeing and health at the forefront when selecting nutritious foods for your diet. It is crucial to keep in mind that nutrition is a journey, and it is critical to choose the path that works best for you, regardless of whether or not that path incorporates gluten.

Chapter 4: Baking Substitutes and Tips

Baking is an art form that requires precision, balance, and a comprehension of the science that lies behind the components of the recipe. Figuring out how to navigate the world of alternative flours and binders is absolutely necessary for those who either suffer from gluten intolerance or choose to lead a lifestyle that is gluten-free. In this extensive guide, we will investigate the art of baking with gluten-free flours, offer advice on getting the ideal texture and structure, and look into the utilization of vital binders such as xanthan gum. Together, these topics will comprise the gluten-free baking guide.

Making Substitutions in Baking with Gluten-Free Flour:

1. **Understanding Gluten-Free Flours:**
    - Flour that does not contain gluten can be made from a variety of different ingredients, including rice, almonds, coconut, sorghum, and chickpeas. Because every type of flour has a distinct taste, mouthfeel, and nutritional profile, it is essential to select the type of flour that is most appropriate for the dish you are preparing.
    - Rice flour, potato starch, tapioca flour, and xanthan gum are the four ingredients that are often combined to make a gluten-free flour blend.

2. **Blending Flours for Optimal Results:**

- Experiment with several flour mixes to find the one that produces the flavor and consistency you want. In cakes, for instance, using a combination of almond flour and coconut flour can provide a crumb that is both moist and delicate.

- Remember that gluten-free flours tend to absorb more liquid than standard wheat flour does, so keep that in mind. Make the necessary adjustments to the amount of liquid called for in your recipe.

3. **Adding Nutritional Value:**

    - There is a possibility that gluten-free flours will not have the same level of nutritional value as whole wheat flour. You can improve the food's nutritional profile by adding in some ground flaxseed, chia seeds, or quinoa flour, among other things.

Tips for Achieving the Right Texture and Structure:

1. **Balancing Moisture:**

    - Baked foods that do not contain gluten typically have a lower moisture content than their equivalents that do contain gluten. Include things that will add moisture to the mixture, such as applesauce, yogurt, or additional eggs.

    - When making gluten-free cookies, using a larger ratio of fat can also contribute to the treats' moisture content and suppleness.

2. **Utilizing Binding Agents:**
   - Binding agents are essential in gluten-free baking since gluten's role in creating structure must be replaced by something else. Binders include ingredients such as psyllium husk, guar gum, and xanthan gum.
   - Particularly useful in this regard is xanthan gum, which may successfully mimic the flexibility of gluten. It should be used in moderation because an excessive amount might cause the texture to become sticky.

3. **Incorporating Eggs:**
   - Eggs have a natural ability to bind ingredients together, which plays a role in the overall structure of baked items. To strengthen the binding, you might want to try adding an additional egg or "eggs" made from flax or chia seeds.

4. **Exploring the World of Starches:**
   - It is possible to improve the texture of gluten-free baked goods by including starches such as arrowroot, tapioca, or potato starch in the recipe. These starches make the texture lighter and fluffier, which is a result of their contribution.

Using Xanthan Gum and Other Binders:
1. **Xanthan Gum:**

- Xanthan gum is a polysaccharide that mimics the properties of gluten. It is effective in small amounts, usually around 1/4 to 1/2 teaspoon per cup of gluten-free flour.
- Gradually add xanthan gum to the dry ingredients while whisking to prevent clumping. Ensure thorough mixing for even distribution.

2. **Guar Gum:**
   - Similar to xanthan gum, guar gum is a natural thickening agent. It is often used in gluten-free recipes for its ability to improve texture and provide stability.
   - Use guar gum in a 1:1 ratio with xanthan gum or according to the recipe's specifications.

3. **Psyllium Husk:**
   - Psyllium husk, derived from the seeds of the Plantago ovata plant, is a soluble fiber that can be used as a binder in gluten-free baking.
   - When using psyllium husk, follow the recommended ratio provided in the recipe, as excessive amounts can lead to a gel-like consistency.

The art of gluten-free baking can be mastered by carefully selecting the appropriate flours, gaining an understanding of the function of binders, and putting into practice key suggestions for achieving the desired texture and structure. You can produce gluten-free baked items that are on par with their conventional equivalents by experimenting with different flour mixtures, ingredients that increase the amount of moisture, and binding agents such as xanthan gum. The world of gluten-free baking is one that, with little effort, experimentation, and ingenuity on your part, can provide delicious and gratifying results.

Chapter 5: Breakfast Recipes

1. Vegetables with Hash Browns

- Prep: 10 minutes
- Cook : 20 minutes
- Servings: 5

Ingredients

- Canola oil, 15 ml
- 4 beaten eggs
- Hash browns, 7 oz.
- Shredded low-fat cheese, 4 ounces
- 2.5 ml of Chile flakes, 1 small onion, and diced

Directions

1. After heating up the oil in the pan, add the onion and hash browns. The combination cooked for a total of five minutes.
2. Simmer for five minutes on low heat after adding the carrots and peppers.
3. Once that's done, stir in the eggs, cheese, and pepper and bake for 10 minutes.
4. Add the parsley and heat, stirring, for an additional 10 seconds.

Nutrition :

- Calories: 290;
- Carbohydrates: 18.9g;
- Protein: 11.8g;

2. Waffles with Cinnamon

- Prep Time: 10 minutes
- Cook Time: 10 minutes
- Serves: 6

Ingredients

- 120g blanched almond flour
- A pinch of salt
- 5g of baking soda
- 4 eggs
- 30g honey
- 5g vanilla extract
- Cooking spray
- 2.8g cinnamon, depending on your taste preference

Directions

1. Before using the waffle maker, preheat it and spray it with cooking spray.
2. Almond flour, baking soda, and salt should all be combined in a bowl. Blend thoroughly.
3. Whisk together the egg whites, honey, and vanilla extract in a separate basin.
4. Once the wet ingredients have been incorporated in the recipe, thoroughly mix the dry ones with them.
5. The waffle iron should have batter poured into it. Cook until the meat turns a golden brown.
6. Butter, maple syrup (or brown rice syrup for a healthier alternative), and a selection of fresh fruits are all delicious toppings for waffles.

Nutrition

- Calories: 488;
- Total fat: 29g;
- Total carbs: 38g;

3. Golden Blueberry Muffins

- Prep Time: 5 minutes
- Cook Time: 25 minutes
- Serves: 12

Ingredients

- 400g blanched almond flour
- 2 eggs
- 2 egg whites
- 250ml honey or maple syrup
- 2.8g baking soda
- 17g apple cider vinegar
- 2.8g salt
- 5g vanilla extract
- 15ml olive oil
- 250g blueberries

Directions

1. Raise the oven's temperature to 350 degrees. Line a standard 12-cup muffin tin with foil or paper liners, then coat the tin with cooking spray. Another option is to use paper liners.
2. With the exception of the blueberries, put all of the ingredients in a food processor or mixer. Blend until no lumps remain.
3. Stir the blueberries into the batter with a wooden spoon.
4. Pour the batter into the muffin tin until it reaches about three-quarters of the way.
5. Bake for 20 to 25 minutes, or until the cookies have gone a golden brown and a toothpick inserted into the center of one comes out clean.

Nutrition

- Calories: 488;
- Protein: 21g;
- Total carbs: 38g;

4. Fluffy Buttermilk Pancakes

- Prep Time: 5 minutes
- Cook Time: 5 minutes
- Serves: 4

Ingredients

- 300g blanched almond flour
- 2.8g baking soda
- 1.4g sea salt
- 3 large eggs, room temperature
- 30g buttermilk
- 17g butter or coconut oil, melted
- 17g pure maple syrup
- 5g pure vanilla extract

Directions

1. Mix sea salt, baking soda, and almond flour in a single basin.
2. Add the buttermilk, eggs, and vanilla extract at this point. Add the buttermilk in a slow, steady stream until the batter reaches the desired texture.
3. Melt some butter or coconut oil over medium heat in a skillet or on a griddle. Next, fill the pan with a large soup spoonful of batter.
4. Cook each pancake for two to three minutes on each side, or until golden brown on both sides and bubbles start to appear. Continue this process with the remaining batter.
5. Pancakes taste great topped with butter, maple syrup (or, for a healthier option, brown rice syrup), and sliced fresh fruit.

Nutrition

- Total fat: 27g;
- Protein: 11g;
- Total carbs: 46g;

5. Buttery Butter Biscuits

- Prep Time: 5 minutes
- Cook Time: 12 minutes
- Serves: 6

Ingredients

- 500g of blanched almond flour
- 2.8g of salt
- 2.8g of baking soda
- A pinch of cinnamon
- 30g of unsalted butter, cold
- 2 eggs
- 17g of honey

Directions

1. In a larger basin, stir together almond flour, baking soda, cinnamon, and salt.
2. Using a pastry cutter or fork, add the chilled butter and stir until crumbs.
3. In a small bowl, whisk the eggs with a fork until they become slightly foamy, about 30 seconds. Mix the almond flour mixture with the eggs until well blended.
4. After forming the dough into a ball, freeze it for roughly ten minutes.
5. Turn the oven on to 350°F. Apply cooking spray to the cookie sheet to grease it.

Nutrition

- Calories: 498;
- Total fat: 39g;
- Protein: 21g;

Gluten Free Cookbook

6. Tasty Oatmeal Raisin Bars

- Prep Time: 20 minutes
- Cook Time: 20-30 minutes
- Serves: 15 bars

Ingredients

- 300g of rolled oats
- 300g of blanched almond flour
- 2.8g of salt
- 2.8ml of baking soda
- 17g cinnamon
- 34g milled golden flaxseed or wheat germ
- 100g of honey
- 100g of coconut oil or butter, melted
- 1 egg, beaten
- 17g of vanilla
- 400g of raisins, a combo of dried fruits and nuts or chocolate chips

Directions

1. Turn the oven on to 350°F. Coat a 13 x 9-inch pan with butter or cooking oil.
2. In a big bowl, combine rolled oats, almond flour, cinnamon, baking soda, salt, and ground golden flaxseed or wheat germ.
3. Create a well in the middle of the mixture and add the egg, vanilla, coconut oil or butter, honey, and egg. Using your hands, thoroughly combine.
4. Press the mixture evenly into the pan that has been prepared.
5. Bake for twenty to thirty minutes, or until a toothpick inserted into the center comes out clean.

Nutrition

- Calories: 116.
- Total fat: 5g;
- Protein: 6g.

7. Cinnamon Vanilla Banana Bread

- Prep Time: 15 minutes
- Cook Time: 50 minutes
- Serves: 12

Ingredients

- 500g blanched almond flour
- 300g ground cinnamon
- 1.4g ground nutmeg
- 2.8g sea salt
- 5ml baking soda
- 3 eggs
- 200ml honey
- 30ml whole milk yogurt
- 2-3 very ripe bananas, mashed
- 5g vanilla extract
- 30g chopped walnuts

Directions

1. Turn the oven on to 350°F. Spread butter or frying oil in a big bread pan.
2. In a big basin, stir together the almond flour, baking soda, nutmeg, cinnamon, and sea salt.
3. Beat the eggs with a hand blender or an electric mixer in a different bowl.
4. Once thoroughly mixed, add the honey, whole milk yogurt, bananas, and vanilla extract.
5. 200 g of the dry ingredients should be added to the mixture at a time, and each addition should be thoroughly incorporated.

6. The walnuts should be chopped and added with a wooden spoon.

Nutrition:

- Calories: 78Fat: 4 g., Carbs: 13 g.

8. Moist Pumpkin Spice Bread

- Prep Time: 10 minutes
- Cook Time: 35 minutes
- Serves: 12

Ingredients

- 400g blanched almond flour
- 1.4g sea salt
- 5ml baking soda
- 30g cinnamon
- 10g nutmeg
- 5.8g cloves
- 2.4g ginger
- 15g Allspice (or substitute)
- 100g roasted pumpkin or winter squash, mashed
- 3 eggs
- 45ml honey
- 1.4g Stevia drops

Directions

1. Turn the oven on to 350°F. Use cooking oil or butter to grease two mini bread pans or a 5 x 9-inch bread pan.
2. In a larger bowl, thoroughly mix almond flour, sea salt, baking soda, cinnamon, nutmeg, cloves, ginger, and allspice.
3. In a second bowl, use an electric mixer or hand blender to combine the eggs, honey, pumpkin or winter squash, and Stevia drops until creamy.
4. 200 g of the dry ingredients should be added to the mixture at a time, and each addition should be thoroughly incorporated.

5. Fill the bread pan or the two smaller bread pans with batter.

6. Bake for 35 minutes, or until a toothpick inserted into the center comes out clean, depending on how hard the center is.

7. Take out of the oven and place on a wire rack to cool fully.

Nutrition
- Calories: 282
- Carbs: 26g
- Fat: 14g.

9. Coffee and Cream Pops

- Prep: 10 minutes
- Cook : 5 minutes
- Servings: 4

Ingredients:

- 10g espresso powder (or to taste)
- 400ml canned coconut milk
- 2. 8g vanilla extract
- cinnamon
- 3g packets Stevia

Directions:

1. In a medium saucepan, boil all ingredients over medium-low heat, stirring regularly, until the espresso powder dissolves fully, about 5 minutes.
2. Transfer the blend into four frozen pop molds. Before serving, freeze for six hours.

Nutrition:

- Calories: 225
- Fat: 24 g.
- Protein: 2 g.

Chapter 6: Lunch Recipes

10. Gluten-Free Angel Food Cake

- Servings: 10-12

Ingredients:

- 600 g egg whites (about 10-12 large eggs)
- 600 g granulated sugar, divided
- Sifted gluten-free cake flour equal to 500 g
- 2 g salt cream of tartar
- 5 g vanilla extract
- You can serve it with fresh fruit and whipped cream (optional)

Preparation:

1. Set kiln temperature to 175 degrees Celsius (or 350 degrees Fahrenheit).
2. In a dish, combine 200 g granulated sugar, salt, and gluten-free cake flour.

3. In a separate bowl, whisk together the egg whites, cream of tartar, and vanilla essence.

4. Add the remaining sugar a bit at a time while beating the egg whites until they attain a stiff peak.

5. To blend the flour mixture with the egg whites, gently fold it in. Take care not to blend too much.

6. Spoon batter into an angel food cake pan.

7. Roast it on a dry sheet pan at 350 degrees for 35 to 40 minutes, or until the top is browned and a skewer inserted in the center comes out clean.

8. To cool, turn the cake out onto a wire rack.

9. After the cake cools, loosen the edges carefully to remove it from the pan.

10. If preferred, top portions of the gluten-free angel food cake with whipped cream and fresh fruit.

11. Gluten-Free Strawberry & Pistachio Olive Oil Cake

- Servings: 8-10

Ingredients:

- 500 g gluten-free all-purpose flour
- parching powder
- 5 g salt 2 large eggs +
- 1 egg yolk
- Sugar, Granulated, 500 g
- 200 g of pure olive oil
- 200 g milk (dairy-free milk can be used as a substitute)
- 200 g of chopped strawberries
- 80 g chopped pistachios Whipped cream and additional strawberries/pistachios, for serving (optional)

Preparation:

1. Concoct kiln for parching at 350 degrees Fahrenheit (175C). Get ready a cake pan that's 9 inches in diameter by greasing and flouring it with gluten-free flour.
2. In a large bowl, combine the gluten-free flour, parching powder, and salt and whisk until smooth.
3. In a separate bowl, whisk the granulated sugar with the eggs and egg yolks to lighten their consistency. Olive oil should be added gradually while beating.
4. Start with the flour concoction and end with the flour as you add it to the egg concoction in alternating portions. Combine in a dish with a little amount of stirring.

5. Mix in the pistachios and strawberry chunks.
6. The cake batter should be poured into the pan and leveled. To test doneness, insert a skewer into the center and remove it cleanly after 30–35 mins in a preheated kiln.
7. After letting the cake rest for 10min in the pan, flip it out onto a wire rack to cool completely.
8. Sprinkle extra chopped strawberries and pistachios over the cake once it has cooled. If you like, you can top it with whipped cream.

12. Gluten-Free Thumbprint Cookies

- Servings: 18-20

Ingredients:

- 500 g unsalted butter
- softened 150 g granulated sugar
- 1 large egg 5 g vanilla extract
- 350 g gluten-free all-purpose flour
- 2 g salt
- 200 g raspberry jam Powdered sugar for garnish

Preparation:

1. Turn the temperature up to 175 degrees (or 350 degrees Fahrenheit). Make a parching sheet with parchment paper.
2. In a mixing dish, cream the sugar and softened butter until light and fluffy.
3. Add the egg and vanilla essence, then beat until well combined.
4. Mix the salt and gluten-free all-purpose flour separately. Till a dough forms, gradually stir in the dry ingredients with the liquid.
5. Form the dough into balls with a diameter of approximately one inch and arrange them on the parching sheet.
6. Press your thumb or the back of a wooden spoon into the center of each biscuit to create a small indentation.
7. Put some raspberry jam within each indentation.
8. In a hot kiln, dry-roast the cookies for 15 to 18 minutes to produce a light golden color on the edges.

9. Take them out of the kiln after five minutes and place them on a wire rack to cool fully.

10. After the thumbprint cookies have cooled, dust them with powdered sugar.

13. Chewy Lemon Sugar Cookies

- Servings: 12-15 cookies

Ingredients:

- Softened 200 g of unsalted butter
- 500 g sugar
- 1 large egg
- 30 g fresh lemon juice
- 15 g lemon zest
- 200 g all-purposeflour
- 2.5 g of Parching Powder
- 1.5 g-of parching soda
- A Pinch.of.Salt
- Powdered sugar, for garnish (optional)

Preparation:

1. Reduce the heat to 350 degrees Fahrenheit in the kiln (175 degrees Celsius). A parching sheet lined with parchment paper is ready to go.
2. Butter and sugar should be creamed together in a large bowl.
3. Combine the egg, lemon juice, and lemon zest by beating all three together.
4. Separately, in a very large mixing bowl, whisk together the flour, parching powder, parching soda, and salt.
5. The dry ingredients should be added to the wet ones gradually until a cohesive dough forms.

6. Roll the dough into 1-inch balls and place on the parching pan.
7. To bake, choose a middle rack and set the timer for 11–14mins..
8. After 5mins., remove the cookies from the parching pan to a wire rack to cool completely.
9. After they have cooled, dust them with powdered sugar and serve.

14. Peanut Butter Blossoms

- Servings: 24 pcs

Ingredients:

- 100 g of room-temperature unsalted butter
- 200 g creamy peanut butter
- 100 g of white sugar
- About a third of a mug of mild brown sugar
- 1 large egg
- Exactly one vanilla extract
- 1,5 kg bread flour
- Parching soda, one teaspoon
- A Pinch of Salt
- 24 Hershey's Kisses, unwrapped

Preparation:

1. Increase the kiln temperature to 350 degrees F. (175 degrees Celsius). A parching sheet should be lined with parchment paper.
2. Mix the sugars (both granulated and brown) with the butter and peanut butter till fluffy.
3. Mix in the egg and vanilla extract.
4. Separately, combine the dry ingredients (flour, parching soda, and salt).
5. To make a dough that holds together, gradually add the dry ingredients to the wet, mixing after each addition.
6. Roll the dough into balls and place them on the parching sheet, spacing them about an inch apart.

7. Dry-roast for 7-10mins or until a little browning occurs around the edges.

8. While still warm, press a Hershey's Kiss into the center of each cookie as soon as you take them out of the kiln.

9. After 5mins, remove the cookies from the parching pan to a wire rack to cool completely.

15. Easy Strawberry Tart

- Servings: 8

Ingredients:

- 500 g flour for all purposes
- 80 g of white sugar
- salt
- 200 g unsalted butter, chilled and cubed
- 200 g heavy cream
- Eight ounces of softened cream cheese
- 100 g of white sugar
- Exactly one vanilla extract teaspoon
- 455g of fresh strawberries, hulled and halved
- 30 g strawberry jam
- Fresh mint leaves for garnish (optional)

Preparation:

1. Add the sugar, salt, and flour to a food processor and pulse until combined.
2. Pulse the concoction until it resembles coarse bread crumbs, then mix in the butter.
3. Press concoction into 9-inch tart pan.
4. Roast at 350 degrees for 20-25 mins.
5. Light peaks should form when you beat heavy cream.
6. Cream cheese, sugar, and vanilla extract should be beaten until combined.
7. Whisk the cream cheese until creamy, then fold in the whipped topping.
8. Fill the cooled crust with the mixture.

9. Top with strawberries and drizzle with warm strawberry jam.
10. Chill for 20-30 mins before serving.
11. Garnish with fresh mint leaves, if desired.

16. Lemon Tart

- Servings: 8

Ingredients:

Crust:

- 500 g all-purpose flour
- 100 g of unsalted butter, cubed
- 80 g of white sugar
- A Pinch of Salt
- Egg Yolk, One

Filling:

- 200 g fresh lemon juice
- 15 g lemon zest
- Sugar, Granulated, Half a Mug
- Three large eggs
- 120 g light cream

Preparation:

1. Adjust the kiln's temperature to 350°F (175 degrees Celsius).
2. Using a food processor, pulse the flour, butter, sugar, salt, and egg yolk until the mixture resembles coarse crumbs to produce the crust.
3. Filling should be pressed into bottom and up sides of tart pan.
4. Wait until the top turns golden, about 15 to 20 minutes. Wait for it to cool before eating.
5. Lemon juice, lemon zest, sugar, eggs, and heavy cream are combined in a mixing dish and whisked together.

6. To use, simply pour the filling into the cooled crust.
7. To ensure the filling is set, dry-roast for 30-35 mins.
8. Wait until the tart has cooled down before serving.

17. Chocolate Tart

- Servings: 8

Ingredients:

Crust:

- 180 g of regular flour
- 80 g of cocoa powder, sugar-free
- salt
- 200 g unsalted butter, cold and cubed
- 80 g granulated sugar
- 1 egg yolk

Filling:

- 500 g of full-fat cream
- Chocolate, 8 ounces bittersweet, chopped
- Softened butter equal to 80 g of unsalted
- Exactly 5 g vanilla extract
- A Hint of Salt

Preparation:

1. Raise the kiln temperature to 350 °f (175 degrees Celsius).
2. Pulse the flour, cocoa powder, salt, butter, sugar, and egg yolk together in a food processor until the concoction resembles coarse crumbs.
3. Spread the concoction into a tart pan and pack it firmly up the edges.
4. To get a light golden color, dry-roast for 15-20 mins. Let it cool down first.

5. Heavy cream should be heated over moderate heat in a small pot.

6. Remove from heat and fold in butter, vanilla, salt, and chocolate chips. Leave it alone for 2 mins.

7. Stir until everything is smoothly combined and pour into the cooled crust.

8. Put in the fridge and let it chill for at least 30 mins.

18. Butter Tarts

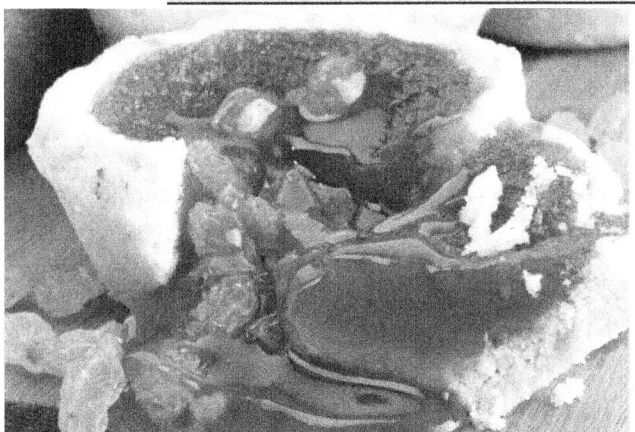

- Servings: 12

Ingredients:

- 200 g unsalted butter, softened
- 200 g brown sugar, packed
- 200 g corn syrup
- 2 eggs
- 5 g vanilla extract
- 2 g salt
- 200 g raisins
- 12 unbaked tart shells

Preparation:

9. Set up a kiln to 190C, or 375F.
10. In a dish, cream the butter and brown sugar together.
11. Add the egg, corn syrup, vanilla, and salt and stir.
12. Add the raisins and fold.

13. The unbaked tart shells should be placed on a parching sheet.

14. Evenly distribute the filling among the twelve tart shells.

15. Allow the filling to set and the crust to turn golden brown in the kiln, about 15 to 20 minutes.

16. Do not try to remove the tarts from their shells until they have cooled.

19. Mini S'mores Tarts

- Servings: 12

Ingredients:

- 500 g of crushed graham crackers
- 80 g melted unsalted. Butter 30 g sugar
- 500 g semisweet chocolate chips
- 200 g heavy cream
- 1.5 g vanilla extract
- Mini marshmallows
- Crushed graham crackers
- Milk chocolate chips

Preparation:

1. Crumb graham crackers, then mix in the butter and sugar. Fill tart pan by pressing in the mixture.
2. Dry-roast for 5-6 mins at 350 degrees Fahrenheit. Frigid Crust.
3. Heat cream in a pot. Add chocolate chips and vanilla. Stir and pour into crusts.
4. Top with mini marshmallows, graham crackers, and milk chocolate chips.
5. To get the marshmallows to a nice golden color, dry-roastfor another 5 to 7 mins.
6. Hold off on removing from pan until it has cooled..

20. Caramel Apple Tart

- Servings: 8

Ingredients:

- 1 defrosted puff pastry sheet
- Two washed and sliced apples
- 80 g-sugar
- 15 g unsalted butter
- 2 g ground cinnamon
- 80 g caramel sauce
- Granulated sugar, used for sprinkling

Preparation:

1. Increase the kiln temperature to 375 degrees F. (190 degrees Celsius).
2. It's best to use a parchment-lined parching sheet when parching with puff pastry.
3. Place the apple slices decoratively atop the puff pastry.
4. Over moderate heat, combine the granulated sugar and butter in a small saucepan.
5. Stir in the ground cinnamon.
6. Dollop the compound onto the apple slices.
7. Put the crust in the kiln and dry-roast for 25 to 30 mins., or until the edges are golden and puffy.
8. Take it out of the kiln, and then pour caramel sauce all over it.
9. Allow it to cool before dusting with powdered sugar.

21. Summer Berry Tortilla Tart

- Servings: 8

Ingredients:

- 2 large flour tortillas
- 30 g melted butter
- 30 g of Granulated Sugar

Filling:

- 8 ounces cream cheese, softened.
- 80 g powdered sugar
- 4 ounces Cool Whip, thawed Topping:
- 200 g mixed berries (strawberries, blueberries, raspberries)
- 15 g honey

Preparation:

1. Increase the kiln temperature to 350 degrees F. (175 degrees Celsius).
2. Brush the tortillas with the melted butter, then sprinkle the sugar over the top. Cut a piece of parchment paper in half and have a parching sheet ready.
3. Cook for 12 mins, or until a golden hue has formed. Wait until they are completely cool before putting them together.
4. Cream cheese and powdered sugar should be mixed together in a separate dish and beaten until smooth. Combine the Cool Whip with a gentle folding motion.

5. In a 9-inch tart pan, arrange four of the cooled tortilla quarters so that they overlap in the center and press tightly against the sides to form a crust edge.

6. To fill the well of a tart pan, place four tortilla quarters in a single layer. Evenly pour the cream cheese concoction over the tortillas using a spoon or offset spatula.

7. Top the filling with fresh mixed berries and honey, if you like.

8. Serve cold or at room temperature after chilling in the fridge for at least 30 mins.

22. Gluten-Free Strawberry-Almond Tart

- Servings: 8

Ingredients:

Crust:

- Almond flour, about 300 g
- 80 g of white sugar
- salt
- 60 g unsalted butter, melted

Filling:

- 8 ounces of softened cream cheese
- Powdered sugar, 200 g
- Exactly one vanilla extract teaspoon
- 500 g sliced strawberries

Preparation:

1. Raise the kiln temperature to 350 degrees F. (175 degrees Celsius).
2. Almond flour, sugar, salt, and melted butter should be mixed together in a dish.
3. Fill a tart pan with the ingredients and pack it firmly up the edges.
4. To get a light golden color, dry-roast for 12-15 mins.
5. Wait until the crust has cooled.
6. Cream cheese, confectioners' sugar, and vanilla extract are mixed together and beaten until smooth.

7. Spread the concoction into the cooled crust.
8. Layer the cream cheese concoction with the cut strawberries.
9. Refrigerate it for at least 30 mins. before serving.

23. Gluten-Free Vegan Matcha Mousse Tart

- Servings: 8

Ingredients:

For the crust:

- 300 gs almond flour
- 80 g maple syrup
- 80 g melted coconut oil Pinch.of.salt

For the matcha mousse filling:

- 14 oz can of full-fat coconut milk
- Approximately 80 g of maple syrup
- 15 g of matcha powder
- 1.5 g almond extract Sprinkle of salt

Preparation:

1. Set kiln temperature to 175 degrees Celsius (or 350 degrees Fahrenheit).
2. Throw the almond flour, maple syrup, melted coconut oil, and a dash of salt into a dish and mix until everything is evenly distributed. Incorporate all of the ingredients together.
3. In a tart pan evenly press the concoction into the bottom and up the edges. Place in a preheated kiln at 350 degrees for 10 to 12 mins..
4. Make the matcha mousse filling while the crust bakes. The solid coconut cream from the coconut milk can should be removed and placed in a separate dish (leaving the liquid behind). Use an electric mixer to

whip the coconut milk until it reaches a creamy consistency.

5. Maple syrup, matcha powder, vanilla essence, and a bit of salt are folded into the whipped coconut cream. Mix everything up well.

6. The matcha mousse filling should be distributed evenly over the crust after it has cooled.

7. Keep the tart cold for at least an hour, or until the mousse has set.

8. Before serving, you can garnish the tart with additional matcha powder, coconut flakes, or fresh berries if desired.

24. Cherry-Almond Vanilla Cupcakes

- Servings: 12 Cupcakes

Ingredients:

- 1 and 0.5mugs all-purpose flour
- 5 g parching powder
- 2 g parching soda
- 2 g salt
- 200 g unsalted butter, softened
- 500 g granulated sugar
- 2 large eggs
- 10 g almond extract
- 200 g whole milk
- 200 g diced cherries (fresh or frozen)
- 200 g unsalted butter, softened
- 500 g sugar
- 30 ml whole milk
- 5 g vanilla extract
- 2 g almond extract
- Sliced almonds and fresh cherries for garnish

Preparation:

9. After setting the kiln temperature to 350F (175C), fill the muffin tins with liners.
10. Mix the flour, soda, powdered salt, and parching powder together.

11. Beat the sugar and butter separately until light and creamy.
12. Whisk in the almond essence and eggs.
13. Mix the dry ingredients with the milk until well combined.
14. Add a few chopped cherries and stir.
15. After filling the cupcake tins, bake them for 20 to 25 minutes.
16. In a mixing dish, combine the butter, powdered sugar, milk, almond extract, and vanilla; whisk until smooth.
17. After the cupcakes cool, decorate them with buttercream and sprinkle almonds and cherry slices on top.

25. Lavender-Honey Cupcakes

- Servings: 12 pcs

Ingredients:

- 400 g of all-purpose flour
- 2 g of leavening
- 2 g of parching soda
- 2 g salt
- 200 g unsalted butter
- 200 g granulated sugar
- 2 large eggs
- 1.5 g vanilla extract
- 200 g whole milk
- 15 g dried chopped lavender-flowers
- 30 ml honey
- 200 g unsalted butter, softened.
- 350 g-sugar
- 30 ml whole milk
- 1.5 g vanilla extract
- 5 g dried lavender flowers

Preparation:

18. Place the muffin pan inside the kiln and set the temperature to 350 degrees F. (175 degrees Celsius).
19. In a large bowl, combine the flour, salt, baking soda, and powder.

20. In a separate bowl, mix together the butter and sugar.
21. Mix well after adding the egg and vanilla.
22. Add the wet ingredients to the dry ones in batches, alternating with milk.
23. After mixing in honey and lavender flowers, pour batter into muffin mugs.
24. Roast on a dry surface for 18 to 20 minutes.
25. Blend together butter, powdered sugar, milk, vanilla extract, and desiccated lavender flowers.
26. After the cupcakes cool, top them with lavender frosting.

26. Mochaccino Cupcakes

- Servings: 12 pcs

Ingredients:

- 300 g cake flour
- 5 g dry-roasting-powder
- 1.5 g parching soda
- 2 g salt
- 80 g unsalted butter, softened
- 500 g granulated sugar
- 2 large eggs
- 80 g cocoa powder
- 80 g hot brewed coffee
- 200 g whole milk
- 200 g unsalted butter, softened.
- 500 g powdered sugar
- 30 ml hot brewed coffee

- 30 ml cocoa powder
- Vanilla extract, 5 g; salt, 2.5 g

Preparation:

1. Prepare the batter and place a muffin tray in a kiln that has been prepared to 175 degrees Celsius (350 degrees Fahrenheit).
2. Cake flour, baking soda, parching powder, and salt are combined to make cake.
3. Using a mixer, whip the butter and sugar until they become light and creamy.
4. Pour in the whisked egg.
5. Blend together cocoa powder and hot brewed coffee; add to wet ingredients in batches, alternating between the two.
6. Pour batter into muffin cups.
7. Roast dry for 18 to 20 minutes.
8. Cream together the butter, salt, cocoa powder, vanilla extract, confectioners' sugar, and hot brewed coffee.
9. After the cupcakes cool, decorate each mug cake with mochaccino frosting.

Chapter 7: Dinner Recipes

27. Italian Sauce

This sauce is made without wheat fillers and it's delicious. It gets its flavor from bones and slow simmering. Use as many type bones as you wish – soup marrow, pork and beef ribs, pork necks, chicken backs, etc. This recipe is great over pasta, or it can be used in most tomato-based recipes for an extra flavor boost.

Ingredients:

- 3 lbs. bones with some meat attached. An extra piece of steak is optional.
- 2 large cans tomato sauce
- 1 small can tomato paste
- 250 g red wine
- 3 diced garlic cloves
- 1 large, chopped onion.
- 2 basil leaves
- 15 g. oregano
- A few fresh basils leaves or 15 g. dried basil
- 1 lb. sliced mushrooms, optional.
- Salt and pepper to taste.

Directions:

1. After putting all of the bones in a roasting pan, roast them for 30 minutes at 350 degrees. This will extract as much flavor as possible.
2. Once the bones have cooled down, place them in a 6-quart slow cooker.
3. Stir in all the remaining ingredients.
4. Simmer for 10 to 12 hours on low.

28. Pot Roast

Ingredients:

- 3 lbs. chuck roast
- Salt and pepper to taste
- 50 ml. liquid aminos – this is a substitute for soy sauce
- 3 cubes of gluten-free beef bouillon
- 5 g. paprika
- 1 sliced medium onion

Directions:

1. After seasoning, put the roast in the slow cooker.
2. Combine the liquid aminos with the crumbled beef bouillon.
3. Stir in 15 milliliters of boiling water.
4. Cover beef with bouillon mixture.
5. Place the onion pieces on top of the roast.
6. Simmer for nine to ten hours on low.

29. Corned Beef and Cabbage

No need to wait for St. Patrick's Day to enjoy some delectable corned beef and cabbage. The slow cooking makes this dinner easy to prepare, and it's utterly scrumptious.

Ingredients:

- 2 lbs. small Russet potatoes
- 1/2 lb. cabbage cut into slices
- 1 lb. sliced carrots
- 300 g of peeled pearl onions
- 15 g. red cider vinegar
- 30 ml. butter
- Salt and pepper to taste
- 1 bay leaf
- 1 g. allspice
- 4 lbs. trimmed corned beef brisket
- 1 kg of vegetable broth

Directions:

1. Put all of the ingredients in the slow cooker, starting with the potatoes.
2. Stir in the corned meat.
3. Over the steak, pour the beef broth.
4. Simmer for ten hours on low.
5. Let the brisket sit for approximately 20 minutes on a dish.

30. BBQ Taco Salad

Everyone loves tacos, and this salad gets its flavor from slow simmering ingredients.

Ingredients:

- 1 lb. ground beef
- 500 g well-rinsed pinto beans
- 100 g salsa
- 15 g. BBQ sauce
- 75 g tomato sauce
- 1 minced garlic clove
- 15 g. olive oil
- 30 ml. diced cilantro
- Salt and pepper to taste

Ingredients for Salad:

- 750 g of salad greens
- 100 g diced tomatoes
- 45 g. chopped cooked bacon
- Chili flakes to taste

Directions:

1. Stir after adding each ingredient to the slow cooker.
2. Cook on low for six hours, scraping off any fat and stirring once or twice.
3. Place the tomatoes and lettuce on a platter, then cover with the taco filling.
4. Add the chili flakes and bacon for seasoning.

31. Beef Curry

A savory spicy dish that is totally delicious.

Ingredients:

- 3 lb. chuck-eye roast
- 50 g coconut milk
- 30 ml. red curry paste
- 4 cracked cardamom pods
- 45 g. fish sauce
- 15 g. onion flakes
- 30 ml. red chili
- 15 g. sugar
- 15 g. cumin
- 15 g. coriander
- Dash of nutmeg
- 15 g. ginger
- 50 g chopped cashews
- 50 g chopped cilantro

Directions:

1. Set the cilantro and cashews aside.
2. Mix with the additional ingredient.
3. Simmer for five hours on high.
4. Before serving, sprinkle the cashews and cilantro over top.
5. You might serve this with Basmati rice.

32. Beef Stroganoff

A creamy stroganoff without any canned "cream" soup. The sauce is thickened with cornstarch instead. Serve over rice gluten-free noodles.

Ingredients:

- 1 lb. stew meat
- 250 g sliced mushrooms
- 1 small, diced onion
- 30 ml. cornstarch
- 300 g beef broth
- Salt and pepper to taste
- 3 g. parsley
- 100 g sour cream
- Slice a few green onions to use as garnish.

Directions:

1. In a slow cooker, combine the beef, onions, and mushrooms.
2. Add the salt, pepper, and parsley and stir.
3. Combine the cornstarch and beef broth in a bowl to make a slurry.
4. Cover the meat with the liquid.
5. Simmer for eight hours on low.
6. After adding the sour cream, simmer for an additional fifteen minutes on high.
7. Throw some green onions on top.

33. Beef Stew

This is a rich stew, perfect for weekday dinner. Stew meat can get stringy and tough, but simmering for hours will make this stew melt in your mouth.

Ingredients:

- 2 lbs. stew meat
- 3 lbs. peeled bite-size potatoes
- 1 lb. peeled and sliced carrots
- 1 small, diced onion
- 2 chopped celery stalks
- 300 g beef broth
- 28-oz. can tomato sauce
- 1 diced garlic clove
- 15 g. gluten-free soy sauce
- 10 g. thyme
- 5 g. oregano
- Salt and pepper to taste
- 1 bay leaf
- 15 g. cornstarch

Directions:

1. Put everything in the slow cooker, excluding the cornstarch.
2. Add enough stirring with a large spoon.
3. Simmer for ten hours on low.
4. In a slow cooker, combine the cornstarch and 60 milliliters of water.
5. Simmer for a further 30 minutes.
6. Put on top of rice.

34. Chicken Prepared with Forty-Five Garlic Cloves

Don't be scared off by all that garlic. Slow cooking turns garlic into a sweet, savory delight.

Ingredients:

- 1 whole chicken
- 45 peeled cloves of garlic left whole
- 15 g. thyme
- 30 ml. olive oil
- Salt and pepper to taste
- Rosemary sprigs to garnish

Directions:

1. After giving the chicken a good rinse, pat it dry.
2. Put twenty cloves of garlic inside the bird.
3. In the slow cooker, move the chicken.
4. Rub the olive oil all over the chicken's exterior with your fingers.
5. Add the rosemary and the remaining cloves of garlic.
6. Cook on low for 8 to 9 hours.
7. When removing the chicken from the slow cooker, use caution. It will be incredibly juicy, with the meat falling off the bones.
8. There's going to be cooking oils. After removing the fat, sprinkle it over the chicken.

35. Orange Chicken

This Chinese-restaurant favorite is allergy-free and delicious.

Ingredients:

- 2 lbs. bite-sized chicken pieces
- ½ flour for dredging. Use a gluten-free biscuit mix
- 30 ml. olive oil
- 6 oz. of orange juice concentrate or 50 g orange juice
- 45 g. brown sugar
- 45 g. ketchup
- 5 g. balsamic vinegar
- 5 g. salt
- 10 g. grated ginger

Directions:

1. The chicken pieces should be coated with the gluten-free flour mixture.
2. Brown the chicken for five minutes in a skillet.
3. The chicken should be moved to a slow cooker.
4. Combine all of the remaining ingredients in a bowl. Taste and adjust the seasoning accordingly.
5. To the slow cooker, add the sauce.
6. Simmer on low heat for several hours.
7. Put on top of rice.

36. General Tso's Chicken

This dish has a bit of heat, as you would expect. The chicken is extremely juicy and tender.

Ingredients:

- 2 lb. bite-size chicken pieces
- 10 g. olive oil
- 30 ml. cornstarch
- 3 g. pepper
- A dash of chili flakes
- 30 ml. gluten-free soy sauce
- 50 g gluten-free hoisin sauce
- 30 ml. honey
- 30 ml. cider vinegar
- 15 g. grated ginger
- 2 minced garlic cloves

Directions:

1. In a dish, combine the pepper and cornstarch.
2. The chicken pieces should be dredged into the mixture.
3. For six to eight minutes, brown the chicken pieces in the olive oil.
4. Put the pieces of chicken into the slow cooker.
5. Stir in all the remaining ingredients.
6. Cook for two to three hours on high.
7. Accompany with steaming vegetables or rice. Garnish with some sliced scallions, if you'd like.

37. Spicy Chicken and Quinoa

Lots of spices give this dish a Southwestern kick, and the quinoa keeps it healthy and gluten-free. Adjust the spices to suit your taste.

Ingredients:

- 500 g corn kernels, frozen is fine
- 1 ½ lbs. of chicken breasts
- 1 100 g salsa
- 1 can drained black beans
- 750 g diced tomatoes
- 1 small chopped green chilies with juices
- 5 g. cumin
- 3 g. oregano
- 2 minced garlic cloves
- 250 g chicken broth
- 250 g quinoa
- 75 g chopped cilantro
- Gluten-free tortilla chips
- 1 sliced avocado

Directions:

1. Put the corn in a slow cooker first.
2. Add the salsa, tomatoes, green chilies, beans, and chicken breast on top.
3. Stir in the chicken broth and seasonings. Mix thoroughly.
4. Cook until chicken is cooked, about 7 hours on low.
5. After removing the chicken with a tong, place it on a dish.
6. After rinsing, put the quinoa to the slow cooker.
7. Return the chicken to the slow cooker after shredding it. Mix every component together.

8. Cook for a further 30 minutes on high.
9. Along with the avocado, cilantro, and gluten-free tortilla chips, serve the chicken.

38. Bourbon Chicken

This chicken isn't drunk; it was named after Bourbon Street in New Orleans. Its taste is as saucy as a Mardi Gras and it's perfect served over rice.

Ingredients:

- 1 ½ lbs. boneless and skinless chicken thighs
- 100 g sliced onion
- 100 g gluten-free soy sauce
- 250 g honey
- 75 g ketchup
- 30 ml. canola oil
- 2 minced garlic cloves
- Salt and pepper to taste
- A dash of red pepper flakes
- 30 ml. cornstarch
- 15 g. water

Directions:

1. In a slow cooker, combine all ingredients (except for the cornstarch and water) and mix thoroughly.
2. Cook for eight hours on low.
3. Transfer the chicken to a platter using tongs.
4. To shred the chicken, use a fork.
5. Mix the water and cornstarch together.
6. To the slow cooker, add the shredded chicken and the cornstarch mixture.
7. Cook for a further fifteen minutes on high.

39. Spicy Moroccan Fish

Use any firm fish for this zesty fish dish.

Ingredients for Marinade:

- 4 diced cloves of garlic
- 30 ml. lemon juice
- 30 ml. olive oil
- 5 g. cumin
- 5 g. paprika
- 15 g. cayenne pepper
- 15 g. turmeric
- 5 g cumin

Ingredients for Fish:

- 2 lbs. firm fish such as halibut, sword fish, cod or sea bass

Directions:

1. Mix together all of the marinade ingredients.
2. Fish should be put in a big zip-lock bag.
3. Cover the fish with the marinade.
4. Store in the fridge for six hours.
5. Fill the slow cooker with 45 grams of water.
6. After adding the fish to the slow cooker, discard the marinade.
7. Cook fish for two hours on low heat.
8. Transfer the fish to a dish with care..

40. Lemony Salmon

Salmon can't be beat for great taste and health benefits. Enjoy.

Ingredients:

- 4 salmon fillets
- 100 g lemon juice
- 30 ml. olive oil
- 2 minced garlic cloves
- 5 g. dill
- Salt and pepper to taste
- Fresh dill springs to garnish

Directions:

1. Combine the first five ingredients in a bowl.
2. After putting the salmon in a zip-lock bag, pour the marinade over it.
3. Put the salmon in the fridge for six hours.
4. The salmon should be put in the slow cooker. Discard the marinade.
5. Add salt and pepper to the salmon to season it.
6. Cook for three hours on low.
7. Before serving, if preferred, top salmon with dill sprigs.

41. Louisiana Jambalaya

This Jambalaya packs some Louisiana heat! We omitted the crocodiles, but we hear the chicken tastes remarkably similar. Feel free to adjust the spice to your own taste and will to live.

Ingredients:

- 500 g diced chicken breasts
- 6 oz. sliced smoked sausage such as Andouille
- 1 diced green pepper
- 1 finely chopped onion
- 3 chopped celery stalks
- 250 g sliced mushrooms
- 500 g diced tomatoes
- 5 minced garlic cloves
- 15 g. chopped cilantro
- 750 g chicken broth
- 100 g. tomato paste
- 15 g. olive oil
- 5 g. hot sauce
- 3 g. cumin
- 3 g. cayenne pepper
- 3 g. thyme
- 5-6 large raw, peeled, deveined shrimp
- 500 g Basmati or Jasmine rice

Directions:

1. Combine all the ingredients, excluding the last two, in a slow cooker (shrimp and rice).
2. Mix well to blend.
3. Simmer for three hours on high.
4. Place the rice in the slow cooker along with the shrimp. Cook for an additional forty-five minutes.

Chapter 8: Snack Recipes

42. Bacon-Wrapped Asparagus, Sweet Peppers, And Green Beans

- Serves 6 :
- Prep time: 5 minutes :
- Cook time: 25 minutes

Ingredients

- 45ml extra-virgin olive oil
- 15g yellow mustard
- 1 pound asparagus, woody ends removed
- ¾ pound green beans, ends trimmed
- 2 bell peppers, cut into thin strips.
- 1 pound bacon
- Kosher salt
- Freshly ground black pepper

Directions

1. Set oven temperature to 425°F.
2. Whisk the oil and mustard together in a small dish. Put aside.
3. In a pot, bring the water to a boil. Sauté the green beans and asparagus together for two to three minutes, or until they are soft and bright green. After draining, pat dry.
4. Together, form little bundles out of the vegetables. Place the ends of the bacon on a baking tray and wrap the bacon around the center of each bundle.
5. Sprinkle the vegetable bundles with salt and pepper and pour the mustard mixture over them.

Nutrition

- Total calories: 237;
- Total fat: 17g;

- Carbohydrates: 10g;

43. Creamy Potato Salad

- Serves 12
- Prep time: 5 minutes
- Cook time: 20 minutes

Ingredients

- 4 eggs
- 1⅓ pounds small red potatoes, cut into 1-inch cubes
- 45ml apple cider vinegar
- 2.5ml salt
- 1 celery stalk, chopped
- 1 medium zucchini, chopped
- 8 scallions, chopped
- 125ml mayonnaise
- 32g sour cream
- 10ml prepared horseradish
- 10g yellow mustard
- 5g sugar
- 2.5g freshly ground black pepper

Directions

1. After roughly 15 minutes of hard boiling, peel, cut, and set the eggs aside.
2. Fill a microwave-safe bowl halfway full of potato cubes with water. Microwave for about 6 minutes, or until fork-tender. After draining and allowing them to cool slightly, add salt and vinegar and toss to coat.
3. Gently combine the remaining salad ingredients with the eggs.

Nutrition

- calories: 19,
- fat: 16g,
- Carbohydrates: 10g;

44. Bean Dip

- Serves 6
- Prep time: 5 minutes
- Cook time: 20 minutes

Ingredients

- 1 (16-ounce) can of gluten-free refried beans
- 1 (8-ounce) package of cream cheese, softened
- 64ml sour cream
- 3 scallions, thinly sliced, divided
- 30ml taco seasoning
- 15g shredded Cheddar cheese, divided
- 125g shredded pepper jack cheese, divided
- 2 jalapeños, finely chopped, divided
- Kosher salt
- Freshly ground black pepper
- 64g cherry tomatoes, quartered
- 32g queso fresco, crumbled
- 32g red onion, chopped

Directions

1. Set oven temperature to 350ºF.
2. Combine the beans, half of the scallions and jalapeño, 100 g of each of Cheddar and pepper jack cheese, taco seasoning, and cream cheese and sour cream in a big bowl. Add pepper and salt for seasoning.
3. Place in an ovenproof dish and sprinkle the remaining 100 g of pepper jack and cheddar cheese on top. Bake until the cheese is melted, about 20 minutes.

Nutrition

- calories: 424
- fat: 31g
- Carbohydrates: 19g

45. Cucumber Cups With Sun-Dried Tomato And Cream Cheese

- Serves 8
- Prep time: 20 minutes

Ingredients

- 6 medium cucumbers
- 2 (8-ounce) packages of cream cheese
- 64ml oil-packed sun-dried tomatoes, coarsely chopped
- 32ml fresh basil, coarsely chopped
- 32g kalamata olives, pitted and coarsely chopped
- 45g chopped fresh chives for garnish

Directions

1. Remove the cucumbers' skin in strips, leaving behind alternating skin strips.
2. Slice the cucumbers into rounds that are ½ inch thick. Scoop out the seeds with a spoon, creating a well in the center of each round.
3. Add the olives, basil, sun-dried tomatoes, and cream cheese. Pulse in a food processor until thoroughly combined.
4. Filling should be spooned into a pastry bag with a big tip. Fill the cucumbers with a piping bag. Sprinkle chives on top.

Nutrition

- Total calories: 126
- Total fat: 8g
- Carbohydrates: 12g

46. Confetti Tuna In Celery Sticks

- Serves 10
- Prep time: 20 minutes

Ingredients

- 1 (3-ounce) can chunk light tuna
- 64g shredded carrots
- 64g shredded red cabbage
- 32g shredded zucchini
- 45ml cream cheese softened
- 15ml plain yogurt
- 2.5ml dried basil, crushed
- Kosher salt
- Freshly ground black pepper
- 1 bunch of celery, cut into 4-inch sticks

Direction

1. In a medium bowl, mix together the tuna, carrots, cabbage, and zucchini.
2. Add the yogurt, cream cheese, and basil; season with the salt and pepper.
3. After filling the celery sticks with the mixture, serve.

Nutrition

- Total calories: 38
- Total fat: 2g
- Carbohydrates: 4g

47. Vegetable Dip

- Makes 500 g
- Prep time: 10 minutes

Ingredients

- 125ml sour cream
- 85ml salsa
- 75ml mayonnaise
- 30ml finely chopped scallions
- 30g red bell pepper, finely chopped
- 5g garlic salt
- Mixed vegetable dippers bell peppers, baby carrots, broccoli, cauliflower, grape tomatoes

Directions

1. In a medium bowl, mix together sour cream, salsa, mayonnaise, scallions, bell pepper, and garlic salt.
2. Keep chilled until you're ready to serve.

Nutrition

- Total calories: 278
- Total fat: 25g
- Carbohydrates: 8g

48. Baked Sweet Potato Wedges With Garlic Aioli

- Serves 4
- Prep time: 10 minutes
- Cook time: 20 minutes

Ingredients

- 5ml extra-virgin olive oil, plus 30 g
- 3 large, sweet potatoes
- 2.5g Himalayan salt
- 5 g chipotle powder
- FOR THE AIOLI
- 125g raw cashews
- 90ml water
- 3 or 4 garlic cloves
- 10g Dijon mustard
- Juice of ½ lemon
- Pinch salt

Direction

1. Set oven temperature to 425°F.
2. Use five grams of oil to grease a baking pan.
3. Clean the sweet potatoes, then peel and pat dry. After trimming off any undesirable areas, cut the potatoes into long wedges that are no thicker than one inch. After sprinkling the last 30 g of oil, place them in the pan. Dust with a little amount of chipotle powder and season with salt.
4. Bake for twenty minutes, rotating a couple times to ensure even cooking.

Nutrition

- Total calories: 378
- Total fat: 22g, Carbohydrates: 37g

49. Vegetable Fritters

- Yield: 10 cakes
- Prep time: 15 minutes
- Cook time: 15 minutes

Ingredients

- 1 large carrot, peeled
- 1 zucchini, peeled
- 1 russet potato, peeled
- 1 medium onion, halved and thinly sliced
- 10g sea salt
- 2 large eggs
- Freshly ground black pepper
- 64ml extra-virgin olive oil

Direction

1. Use a spiralizer to chop the zucchini and carrot.
2. Slice the potato into thin strips using a mandolin.
3. In a colander, combine the onion, potato, zucchini, and carrot. Season with salt. Give the veggies a good fifteen minutes to stand. Using a paper towel, pat dry.
4. Whisk the eggs and season with pepper in a different bowl. Add the veggies and toss to coat.
5. A big sauté pan should be heated over medium-high heat. Pour a little oil into the pan.

Nutrition

- Total calories: 131
- Total fat: 12g
- • Carbohydrates: 5g

50. Pistachio Cranberry Energy Bites

- Makes 10 to 12 balls
- Prep time: 15 minutes

Ingredients

- 8 ounces (about 250 g) of dates, chopped
- 64ml honey
- 15g chia seeds
- 15 g ground flax seed
- Pinch salt
- 200g gluten-free old-fashioned oats
- 125g dried cranberries
- 125g shelled pistachios
- 50g chocolate chips

Direction

1. In a blender or food processor, combine the dates, honey, chia seeds, flax seeds, and salt; pulse to mix.
2. After transferring the mixture to a large bowl, whisk in the chocolate chips, oats, cranberries, and pistachios.
3. Shape into golf ball-sized spheres and keep chilled until mealtime.

Nutrition

- Total calories: 299
- Total fat: 9g
- Carbohydrates: 54g

51. Spicy Avocado Dip

- Serves 4
- Prep time: 10 minutes

Ingredients

- 2 large, ripe avocados
- 2 garlic cloves, crushed
- Juice of 1 lime
- 5g chili powder, plus more for serving
- Pinch salt
- Freshly ground black pepper

Directions

1. Place the avocados, garlic, lime juice, and chili powder in a food processor and blend until smooth, about 1 minute. Season with salt, pepper, and additional chili powder, if desired.
2. Transfer to a bowl and garnish with chili powder. Serve with your favorite gluten-free chips or alongside tacos.

Nutrition

- Total calories: 168
- Total fat: 15g;
- Carbohydrates: 9g;

52. Sweet-And-Sour Zucchini

- Serves 4
- Prep time: 15 minutes :
- Cook time: 5 minutes

Ingredients

- 2 large zucchini, thinly sliced into rounds
- 5g salt
- 30 ml peanut oil
- ½ to 1 red chile (depending on your spice tolerance), seeded and sliced into thin strips
- 1 garlic clove, thinly sliced
- 2.5g fresh ginger, minced
- 15ml rice vinegar
- 15ml tamari or gluten-free soy sauce
- 10g sugar
- 10ml sesame oil

Direction

1. Place the zucchini in a large colander, sprinkle with the salt, and cover with a small plate to weigh it down. Let stand for 15 minutes to let moisture out.
2. Quickly rinse the zucchini in cold water. Transfer them to a plate with several paper towels to absorb more moisture.
3. Heat a wok over high heat and add the peanut oil, Chile, garlic, and ginger. Sauté for a few seconds.

Nutrition

- Total calories: 108 Total fat: 8g, Carbohydrates: 9g

53. Sweet Potato Fries

- Prep: 10 minutes
- Cook : 25 minutes
- Servings: 2

Ingredients:

- 1 large, sweet potato
- 5g ground turmeric
- 5g ground cinnamon
- Salt & ground black pepper
- 30ml extra-virgin olive oil

Directions:

1. Arrange a baking tray having foil paper.
2. In a sizable bowl, add all ingredients and toss to coat well.
3. Transfer the mixture to the prepared baking sheet.
4. Bake for around 25 minutes, flipping once after 15 minutes.
5. Serve immediately.

Nutrition:

- Calories: 211 Fat: 14g
- Carbohydrates: 23g
- Fiber: 6g
- Protein: 4g

54. Okra Fries

- Prep: 15 minutes
- Cook : 35 minutes
- Servings: 4

Ingredients:

- 30ml olive oil, divided.
- 45g creole seasoning
- 2.5g ground turmeric
- 5ml water
- 1-pound okra, trimmed and slit in the middle

Directions:

1. Prepare a baking sheet with foil paper and grease with 15 g of oil.
2. In a bowl, mix creole seasoning, turmeric, and water.
3. Fill the slits of okra with turmeric mixture.
4. Place the okra onto the prepared baking sheet in a single layer.
5. Bake for 30-35 minutes, flipping once inside a middle way.

Nutrition:

- Calories: 198
- Fat: 10g
- Carbohydrates: 25g
- Protein: 15g

55. Potato Sticks

- Prep: 15 minutes
- Cook : 10 min
- Servings: 2

Ingredients:

- 1 large russet potato
- 10 curry leaves
- 1.4ml ground turmeric
- 1.4g red chili powder
- Salt, to taste
- 15ml essential olive oil

Directions:

1. Arrange 2 baking sheets with parchment paper.
2. In a sizable bowl, add all ingredients and toss to coat well.
3. Transfer the amalgamation to the prepared baking sheets in a single layer.
4. Bake for around 10 minutes
5. Serve immediately.

Nutrition:

- Calories: 187
- Fat: 9g
- Carbohydrates: 26g
- Protein: 14g

56. Zucchini Chips

- Prep: 15 minutes
- Cook : 15 minutes
- Servings: 2

Ingredients:

- 1 medium zucchini, cut into thin slices
- 8g ground turmeric
- 8g ground cumin
- Salt, to taste
- 10ml essential olive oil

Directions:

1. Arrange 2 baking sheets with parchment paper.
2. Put all the fixing, then mix to coat well in a large bowl.
3. Transfer a combination into prepared baking sheets in a single layer.
4. Bake for approximately 10-fifteen minutes
5. Serve immediately.

Nutrition:

- Calories: 181 Fat: 10g Carbohydrates: 17g Protein: 24g

57. Beet Chips

- Prep: 15 minutes
- Cook : 20 minutes
- Servings: 2

Ingredients:

- 1 beetroot, trimmed, peeled, and sliced thinly
- 5g garlic, minced
- 5g Nutrition:
- yeast
- 2.5g red chili powder
- 5ml coconut oil, melted

Directions:

1. Put the entire fixing, then toss to coat well in a large bowl.
2. Transfer the mixture to the prepared baking sheet in a single layer.
3. Bake for approximately twenty minutes, flipping once inside the middle way.
4. Serve immediately.

Nutrition:

- Calories: 80 Fat: 4.5g Carbohydrates: 6g Protein: 3g

58. Beet Greens Chips

- Prep: 15 minutes
- Cook : 25 minutes
- Servings: 2

Ingredients:

- 1 large bunch beet greens, tough ribs removed
- Salt & ground black pepper
- Olive oil, as required.

Directions:

1. Arrange a baking sheet having parchment paper.
2. In a sizable bowl, add all ingredients and toss to coat well.
3. Transfer the leaves to the prepared baking sheet inside a single layer.
4. Bake for approximately 25 minutes, flipping once after fifteen minutes.
5. Serve immediately.

Nutrition:

- Calories: 204 Fat: 4g Carbohydrates: 17g Protein: 7g

59. Spinach Chips

- Prep: 10 minutes
- Cook: 8 minutes
- Servings: 1

Ingredients:

- 250g fresh spinach leaves
- Few drops of extra-virgin olive oil
- Salt, to taste
- Italian seasoning, to taste

Directions:

1. Arrange a baking sheet with parchment paper.
2. In a substantial bowl, add spinach leaves and drizzle with oil.
3. With your hands, rub the spinach leaves till al the leaves are coated with oil.
4. Transfer the leaves to the prepared baking sheet in a single layer.
5. Bake for about 8 minutes.
6. Serve immediately.

Nutrition:

- Calories: 200 Fat: 11g Carbohydrates: 12g Protein: 16g

60. Plantain Chips

- Prep: 15 minutes
- Cook : 10 minutes
- Servings: 1

Ingredients:

- 1 plantain, peeled and sliced
- 2.5g ground turmeric
- Salt, to taste
- 5ml coconut oil, melted

Directions:

1. Mix the entire fixing, then coat well in a large mixing bowl.
2. Transfer half of the mixture to a large, greased, microwave-safe bowl.
3. Microwave on high for around 3 minutes.
4. Now, decrease the capacity to 50% and microwave for approximately 2 minutes.
5. Repeat with the remaining plantain mixture.

Nutrition:

- Calories: 199 Fat: 9g Carbohydrates: 14g Protein: 8g

Chapter 9: Meal Planning and Batch

Beginning a lifestyle that is gluten-free necessitates careful planning and preparation to create a diet that is both diverse and nutritionally adequate. In this tutorial, we will discuss helpful hints for meal planning that are gluten-free, the skill of cooking in batches, and the convenience of freezing gluten-free recipes. Individuals can simplify their daily routines, save time, and keep a gluten-free diet that is well balanced by adopting these techniques and putting them into practice.

Tips for Planning Gluten-Free Meals:

1. **Diversify Your Gluten-Free Grains:**
   - Although wheat, barley, and rye are not permitted, there is a diverse selection of grains that do not contain gluten that can be consumed. Include quinoa, brown rice, millet, buckwheat, and amaranth in your diet to increase the diversity of your meals and improve their nutritional content.

2. **Prioritize Fresh Fruits and Vegetables:**
   - Fruits and vegetables that are still in their original state do not contain gluten and are a good source of fiber, vitamins, and minerals. To ensure that you are eating a balanced and nutritious diet, center your meals on a variety of colorful fruits and vegetables.

3. **Lean Proteins:**
   - Plan your meals such that they consist of lean proteins like chicken, fish, beans, and other legumes, as well as tofu. These different forms of protein will not only make your diet more interesting but will also help you feel fuller for longer.

4. **Mindful Label Reading:**
   - Gluten is sneaky and can be found in places you wouldn't expect it, such as sauces, dressings, and processed foods. Get into the habit of reading food labels with close attention in order to locate possible sources of gluten.

5. **Experiment with Gluten-Free Flours:**
   - Investigate the world of flours that do not include gluten, such as chickpea flour, almond flour, and coconut flour. These gluten-free alternatives can be used in baking and cooking to make it possible to prepare all of your favorite meals without the presence of gluten.

Batch Cooking and Freezing Gluten-Free Dishes:

1. **Choose Freezer-Friendly Recipes:**
   - Because not all foods are suitable for freezing, it is vital to select recipes that keep their flavor and texture even after being frozen. Cooking in large batches and freezing dishes such as casseroles, stews, soups, and even some types of sauces can be quite beneficial.

2. **Invest in Quality Containers:**
   - For the purpose of storing your batch-cooked meals, you should consider purchasing a wide array of containers that are suitable for freezing. Your food will stay as fresh as possible and won't have freezer burn if you store it in containers made of glass or plastic that is free of the harmful chemical BPA.

3. **Label and Date:**
   - For effective meal planning, accurate labeling is absolutely necessary. In order to keep track of the dish's freshness, clearly mark each container with the dish's name and the date it was prepared. You might want to think about utilizing a rotating system to make sure that older meals are consumed first.

4. **Portion Control:**
   - Before freezing, portion out meals that have been cooked in bulk into portions suitable for individuals or families. This makes it much simpler to defrost only the items that are required, which in turn helps to reduce the amount of food that is wasted.

5. **Meal Prep in Batches:**
   - Schedule certain days of the week for meal preparation and cooking in bulk. This not only helps you save time during the week, but it also enables you to enjoy a wider variety of meals

without the need to worry about preparing each one individually.

Weekly Meal Plans:

1. **Plan Ahead:**
   - Take some time at the beginning of each week to plan your meals. Consider your schedule, activities, and any social events to tailor your meal plan accordingly.

2. **Balance Macronutrients:**
   - Ensure your meals contain a balance of protein, carbohydrates, and healthy fats. This not only supports overall health but also helps maintain energy levels throughout the day.

3. **Incorporate Leftovers:**
   - Strategically plan meals to incorporate leftovers from batch-cooked dishes. For example, roast extra vegetables to use in salads, or cook additional protein for a quick stir-fry the next day.

4. **Variety is Key:**
   - Keep your meals interesting by incorporating a variety of flavors, textures, and cuisines. This helps prevent monotony and ensures you receive a broad spectrum of nutrients.

5. **Snack Smartly:**
   - Plan nutritious gluten-free snacks to curb hunger between meals. Fresh fruit, Greek

yogurt, nuts, and gluten-free granola bars are convenient and satisfying options.

Mastering gluten-free meal planning and batch cooking is a game-changer for those navigating a gluten-free lifestyle. By diversifying your grains, prioritizing fresh ingredients, and experimenting with freezer-friendly recipes, you can save time, reduce stress, and enjoy a wide range of delicious and nutritious meals. Whether you're a seasoned meal prepper or just starting, these strategies can empower you to maintain a gluten-free diet without compromising on taste or variety.

Chapter 10: Troubleshooting and FAQs

Troubleshooting and FAQs for Gluten-Free Living

Living a gluten-free lifestyle can be challenging, but with the right knowledge and strategies, it becomes more manageable. Whether you're new to gluten-free living or have been navigating this dietary choice for some time, here are common challenges, frequently asked questions, and tips for dining out and traveling while gluten-free.

Common Challenges in Gluten-Free Cooking:

1. Flour Substitutes:

- **Challenge:** Traditional wheat flour is a staple in many recipes, and finding the right substitute can be tricky.

- **Solution:** Experiment with alternative flours such as almond flour, coconut flour, rice flour, or a gluten-free flour blend. Each has its unique characteristics, so try different combinations to achieve the desired texture and taste.

2. Texture and Moisture Issues:

- **Challenge:** Gluten provides elasticity and structure to baked goods. Without it, achieving the right texture can be a challenge.

- **Solution:** Add binders like xanthan gum or guar gum to improve the texture. Additionally, using ingredients like applesauce, yogurt, or mashed bananas can enhance moisture in recipes.

3. **Cross-Contamination:**

- **Challenge:** Even trace amounts of gluten can be harmful, and cross-contamination is a significant concern.
- **Solution:** Have a dedicated gluten-free workspace, use separate utensils and cookware, and be cautious when buying pre-packaged items to ensure they are certified gluten-free.

4. **Label Reading:**

- **Challenge:** Gluten hides in many processed foods under different names.
- **Solution:** Learn to read labels carefully. Look for "gluten-free" certifications and be aware of common gluten-containing ingredients like wheat, barley, and rye.

5. **Balancing Nutrients:**

- **Challenge:** Some gluten-free diets may lack certain nutrients found in wheat-based products.
- **Solution:** Incorporate a variety of naturally gluten-free whole foods like fruits, vegetables, lean proteins, and gluten-free grains such as quinoa and brown rice to ensure a balanced diet.

Frequently Asked Questions about Gluten-Free Living:

1. Is Oats Gluten-Free?

- *Answer:* Pure, uncontaminated oats are gluten-free. However, many commercially available oats are processed in facilities that also process wheat, leading to cross-contamination. Look for certified gluten-free oats if you have celiac disease or gluten sensitivity.

2. Can I Consume Alcohol on a Gluten-Free Diet?

- *Answer:* Many distilled spirits are gluten-free, but some alcoholic beverages can contain gluten. Be cautious with beer, as it typically contains gluten. Wine and gluten-free beers or spirits are safer options.

3. Is Gluten-Free the Same as Wheat-Free?

- *Answer:* No. Gluten is a protein found in wheat, barley, and rye. Wheat-free means avoiding wheat, but gluten-free extends to other grains containing gluten.

4. Are Gluten-Free Processed Foods Healthy?

- *Answer:* Not necessarily. Gluten-free processed foods can be high in sugar, unhealthy fats, and low in nutrients. Focus on whole, unprocessed foods for a healthier gluten-free diet.

5. How to Handle Social Situations and Eating Out?

- *Answer:* Communicate your dietary needs clearly, ask about gluten-free options, and choose restaurants with gluten-free menus. It's essential to advocate for your health, and many establishments are accommodating to gluten-free requirements.

Tips for Dining Out and Traveling While Gluten-Free:

1. Research Beforehand:

- Before dining out or traveling, research gluten-free options and restaurants in the area. Apps and websites can provide reviews and recommendations from the gluten-free community.

2. Communicate Effectively:

- When eating out, communicate your dietary needs to the server, chef, or kitchen staff. Emphasize the importance of avoiding cross-contamination.

3. Choose Accommodating Restaurants:

- Opt for restaurants that are known for their gluten-free options or have a dedicated gluten-free menu. This reduces the risk of encountering misunderstandings.

4. Pack Gluten-Free Snacks:

- When traveling, carry gluten-free snacks to avoid being caught hungry without safe food options. This is especially important in places where gluten-free choices might be limited.

5. Learn Basic Phrases in the Local Language:

- If traveling to a region where your primary language isn't spoken, learn basic phrases related to gluten-free needs. This can help you communicate your dietary restrictions more effectively.

6. Consider a Translation Card:

- Create a card in the local language explaining your gluten-free requirements. This can be especially useful in countries where language barriers are significant.

7. Check Airport and Airline Options:

- Airports and airlines are becoming more aware of dietary restrictions. Check in advance for gluten-free meal options, and if needed, bring your snacks on the plane.

8. Stay Informed About Local Cuisine:

- Understand the local cuisine and common ingredients in the region you are visiting. This knowledge can help you make informed choices when dining out.

9. Pack Gluten-Free Essentials:

- In addition to snacks, consider packing essential gluten-free ingredients like gluten-free flour or pasta if you anticipate limited food options.

10. Be Flexible and Patient:

- Despite your best efforts, challenges may arise. Stay flexible, be patient, and have a plan for unexpected situations, such as carrying a list of safe local restaurants or emergency snacks.

Navigating a gluten-free lifestyle requires dedication, but armed with knowledge and preparation, you can enjoy a varied and satisfying diet while minimizing the challenges that may arise. Stay informed, communicate effectively, and embrace the growing availability of gluten-free options both at home and on your travels.

Conclusion

In the culinary adventure that we set out on within the pages of the "Gluten-Free Cookbook," our goal was crystal clear: to help you navigate the maze of gluten-free life by providing a symphony of tastes that goes beyond the confines of dietary restrictions. As we near the end of this gastronomic journey, let us take a moment to pause and contemplate the flavorful tapestry that we have created as well as the newly discovered opportunities that have opened up before us.

This cookbook is a celebration of culinary diversity that shatters conventional preconceptions about how one should live a gluten-free lifestyle. This fundamental truth lies at the heart of this cookbook. We dispelled the myth that following a gluten-free diet is equivalent to living a life of deprivation by focusing on meals that made use of flavorful ingredients and creative cooking techniques. Instead, we have looked at it as a chance to unleash our creative side in the kitchen and embark on a journey where there are no restrictions on how things should taste.

Our investigation started with gaining an understanding of gluten, which included analyzing its function in classic recipes and demystifying the process of switching to a diet that does not include gluten. We explored the broad spectrum of gluten-free flours, illuminating the varied textures and flavors that these flours bring to our culinary undertakings as a result of our exploration. Each ingredient became a stroke on the canvas that is gluten-free gastronomy, from the nutty allure of almond flour to the powerful character of buckwheat flour.

As we moved forward, the cookbook evolved into a haven for people who were looking for comfort in a world where dietary restrictions frequently create a sense of exile from the culinary world. We successfully navigated the complex flavor dynamics, demonstrating that eating gluten-free does not require sacrificing flavor. We went beyond borders, encouraging you to appreciate the richness of flavors from around the world inside the confines of your gluten-free kitchen. These flavors range from the strong spices of the Middle East to the delicate subtleties of Asian cuisine.

The significance of practicing mindful eating arose as a recurrent concept, and its advocates urged us to pay attention not only to the components of the foods we consume but also to the physiological effects of the decisions we make. The recipes that are provided in this article are more than just a collection of instructions; rather, they are a demonstration of the supportive connection that exists between nutrition and wellbeing. It is a rallying cry to reclaim control over our own health without sacrificing the pleasure that comes from enjoying a great meal.

Our objective was not simply to provide a collection of recipes, but rather to offer a holistic guide, a culinary companion that enables you to adopt a gluten-free lifestyle with self-assurance. We hope that we have delivered on this promise. The solution is not only to abstain from consuming foods containing gluten; rather, it is to look forward to the discovery of gluten-free components that can enhance your culinary experience. It's about reveling in the pure pleasure of a well-crafted gluten-free cuisine while appreciating the moment, enjoying the process, and making the most of every bite.

If there is one thing that you should walk away with from our culinary adventure, let it be the knowledge that you are no longer bound by the limitations of having a gluten-centric perspective. The road toward eliminating gluten from one's diet is not one of concession; rather, it is an invitation to rethink one's relationship with food and to take pleasure in the varied symphony of flavors that can be found well beyond the bounds of traditional recipes. It serves as a reminder that confinement is the womb from which invention emerges, and that despite the constraints imposed by a gluten-free diet, a whole new universe of unfathomable opportunities awaits discovery.

When you put the final page in this cookbook, try not to think of it as an ending point but rather as a gateway to a new culinary world. This is a world in which living a gluten-free lifestyle is not a limitation but rather an entry point to a more mindful, flavorful, and enriching method of nourishing oneself and one's loved ones through food. The voyage does not come to an end here; rather, it only transitions into an ongoing investigation of flavors, textures, and the unbounded creativity that can be found within a gluten-free kitchen.

Before we part ways, I want to express how much I appreciate you coming along on this tasty adventure with me. Your gluten-free culinary adventures may be as varied as the recipes contained inside these pages, and may your kitchen continue to serve as a canvas for the artistry of creating a life that is both healthful and tasty. Cheers to a life in which being gluten-free isn't a limitation but rather a celebration of the freedom to experiment with new foods!

Printed in Dunstable, United Kingdom